SPIRIT OF THE CANE
The Story of Cuban Rum

SPIRIT OF THE CANE

The Story of Cuban Rum

by

Anistatia Miller & Jared Brown

Mixellany Limited

All correspondence should be addressed to the publisher's attention at: Mixellany Limited, The White House, Nettleton, Chippenham SN14 7NS United Kingdom.

Photo Credits: Caribe Hilton Hotel archives 171, 172; Getty Images 16, 24, 119, 157; Havana Club SA 6, 28, 60, 62, 64, 66, 67, 69, 73, 74, 80, 115, 116; Jared Brown (photographer) 26-27, 78-79, 83, 85, 89, 90, 91, 95, 107, 120, 122-123, 124, 190-191, 194; Anistatia Miller (photographer) 191; Caleb Krivoshey 206; New York Public Library Digital Collections 19, 20, 22,23, 25, 37, 40; Nigel Cattlin/ Alamy Stock Photo 48

From the authors' personal collections: 10-11, 14, 15, 21, 30, 33, 35, 39, 42, 43, 46, 58-59, 81, 82, 84, 87, 88, 92, 93, 84, 87, 88, 92, 93, 97, 101, 108, 114, 129, 148,161, 170, 181, 198

Public domain: 12,18, 20, 38,41, 44,45, 49,51, 118 180

Sugar cane motif throughout: Shutterstock Images

Text design by Adrian Hodgkins Design

Cover design by Tea Filipi

First edition

British Library Cataloguing in Publication Data Available

Hardcover: ISBN: 978-1-907434-49-5

Softcover: ISBN: 978-1-907434-48-8

CONTENTS

INTRODUCTION

W e have researched the origins of hundreds of drinks and the births of more than a few spirits over the past quarter of a century. In all this time our most ecstatic moments as drink historians have come from delving deep into archives, libraries, and interviews that focus on our two favourite spirits: gin and Cuban rum. We may have first been led down the road to perdition with our fascination in gin and Martinis back in 1995 when we first launched the *Shaken Not Stirred®:A Celebration of the Martini* website and subsequent book. But it was the invitation to visit Havana, in 2008, that set us on a passionate journey of exploration, introspection, and revelation.

The fruits of our initial endeavours were published the following year in *Cuba: The Legend of Rum*. But a year to research, write, and publish a history in collaboration with two additional authors did not sate our natural inclination and we continued digging for more facts, more proof, more myth-busting moments. In the case of Cuban rum, the road to revelation took substantial leaps.

As with the provenance of numerous drinks, we were never satisfied with what was considered to be gospel. The authorship of El Presidente was the first clue, when a subsequent visit to Havana, in 2010, disclosed a new location and indeed a new inventor! Conversations led to scouring the stalls in the Plaza de Armas for copies of Basil Woon's travelogue, tattered cocktails books, postcards, old magazines. Further research online with new search parameters led to even more questions, more digging. We published our findings, in 2012, in the book *Cuban Cocktails*.

This analysis of the most significant classics—Mojito, Cuba Libra, Daiquirí, Piña Colada, and El Presidente—led to a new curiosity. If these drinks possessed DNA that frequently led to foreign influence, what of the spirit itself?

Cuba has an intricately-woven cultural fabric. Every outside influence, whether it be Caribbean, South American, European, Asian, or American, has been embraced and adapted by the island's population. Many of the classic Cuban drinks are predominantly descended from familiar Spanish, French, and even English compounds.

But what of the spirit itself?

We learned that the same holds true for the development of authentic Cuban rum: The inspiration, technology, technique, and passion culled from Spanish, French, Dutch, and British sources were introduced, adapted, and improved on this Caribbean island. And what has been harvested since the early 1800s—this liquid gold—continues to feature in drinks around the world.

Within these pages, you will find the second step in our journey, the culmination of eight years of fact finding and analysis of Cuban rum and the drinks that feature this versatile spirit. The first chapter offers a new understanding of how sugar came to the New World and became a valuable commodity second only to gold. Chapter Two discusses how *aguardiente de caña* was born and how it begat Caribbean rums. It further discusses the lucrative relationship that was established between Cuba sugar planters and the world's largest rum production region prior to Prohibition in the USA: the New England and Mid-Atlantic rum distilleries. Revolutions–political, economic, and industrial—played critical roles in the growth and development of a potential Cuban rum industry from the late 1700s through the mid-twentieth century paint a portrait of how all these puzzle pieces formed the spirit and its growing popularity.

Chapter Three narrates how modern Cuban rum is made, how it differs from its close relations—British- and French-style rums— as well as how to taste and appreciate this highly-accessible spirit.

Chapters Four and Five are dedicated to revising and presenting anew what we now know about Cuba's legendary bars, its bartenders, and the origins of its most famous classic drinks. But history is useless if it is only written as a nostalgic exercise. The way spirits and drinks were made in the past cannot be replicated for a new audience. Our tastes and expectations have evolved with time. The way the spirit is made, the way the secondary ingredients are grown, harvested, and preserved have changed.

So what history does for us is it gives us an opportunity to get the story right so we can proceed into the future with an understanding of the truth as it unfolds. Thus, turning to the future, we offer up what new generations are creating with Cuban rum which goes far beyond the worlds of tiki and tropical.

Are we finished seeking more facets of the intricately-woven fabric that portrays the story of Cuban rum? Probably not. But for now, we invite you to join us along this passionate journey to be inspired by what we have found thus far.

Cuba: Paisaje.
Landscape.

THE NEW WORLD

Chapter One

Columbus Discovers Cuba and Its People

A verdant crest rises low above nurturing blue seas. Who knows what it is? Perhaps it's the tip of a continent. Perhaps it's an island. A lush forest curtain shrouds the horizon in rich emerald green. Warm fragrances of sweet and spice waft from a thickly humid jungle. Multitudes of birds raise a chorus of song. Unassuming tribal natives emerge naked onto the beach, running to behold the Spanish carrack *Santa Maria* and its companion caravels *Niña* and *Pinta*. This is the Garden of Eden. This is Cuba.

It is Sunday, 28 October 1492. The Genoese explorer Christopher Columbus is bedazzled by this vision of paradise. He writes in his journal: "It is the most beautiful island ever seen…"[1]

Columbus is convinced that this land is the eastern frontier of the Great Khan's empire of Cathay. No one on board his sailing fleet knows that an enormous continent—a new world—separates the Orient from Europe across the Atlantic Ocean. No one guesses that this landfall is the largest body in an archipelago of more than 4,000 islands and keys that are loosely strung along the edge of the Tropic of Cancer that rims the Gulf of Mexico. In a few years, Europeans will call this region the Caribbean, the Antilles, the West Indies.

---

1   G.L. Simons, *Cuba: From Conquistador To Castro* (1st edn, St Martin's Press 1996) 79.

First Encounters

B ut no, this new land is not Chipangu—the poetic name that the Venetian merchant-explorer Marco Polo attributed to the island empire of Japan. But that is what Columbus at first believed. Rustichello of Pisa recorded, in 1298, Polo's recollections of Chipangu that: "...the quantity of gold they have is endless; for they find it in their own Islands and the King does not allow it to be exported. Moreover few merchants visit the country because it is so far from the main land and thus it comes to pass that their gold is abundant beyond all measure."[2] Those visions, documented in Polo's memoir *Il Millione*, [*see below*] echoed in Columbus's mind as he first set sight upon this land.

Gold was the treasure that lured European rulers to the exotic kingdoms of the Orient. Emissaries were sent across the Silk Routes by land and by sea. Gold was the reason that Spain's King Ferdinand II of Aragon and Queen Isabella I of Castile commissioned Columbus to seek a new and considerably faster passage to the Orient by navigating due west across the Atlantic Ocean.

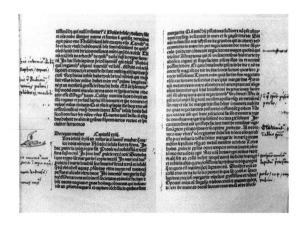

Upon reaching San Salvador—in what is now The Bahamas—Columbus and his crew heard tales about a neighbouring land further west. He remarked: "I have heard these people say that [Cuba] was very large and of great traffic and that there were in it gold and spices and great ships and merchants. And they showed me that

---

2   Marco Polo, Henry Yule and Henri Cordier, *The Travels Of Marco Polo* (1st edn, Dover Publications 1993) 253

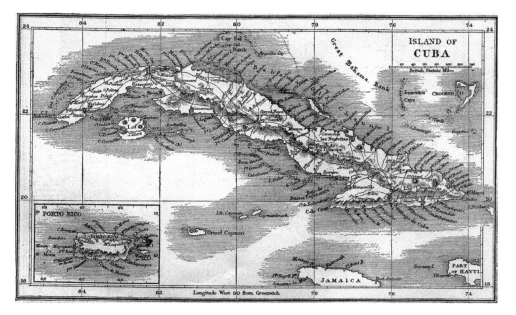

I should go to it by the west-southwest and I think so. For I think
that if I may trust the signs which all the Indians of these islands
have made me and those whom I am carrying in the ships, for by the
tongue I do not understand them, [Cuba] is the Island of Chipangu,
of which wonderful things are told and on the globes which I have
seen and in the painted maps, it is in this district."[3]

In fact, Columbus was so thoroughly convinced unto his dying
day that the land was so vast that Cuba was a peninsula, part of a
large continent. [see above] On 1 November 1492, he recorded in
his journal that: "…it is certain that this is the mainland and that I
am before Zayto and Guinsay, a hundred leagues more or less from
both of them and this is clearly shown by the tide, which comes in a
different manner from that in which it has done up to this time; and
yesterday when I went to the northwest I found that it was cold."[4]

3   Edward Everett Hale, *The Life Of Christopher Columbus From His Own Letters And
Journals* (1st edn, University of Virginia Library 1999). 52

4   Hale, p 54. Zayto is also known as Zaitun or Xuntain, which is in Quangzhou prefec-
ture in China. Guinsay or Quinsay was Polo's loan word from the Persian term for "capital".
According to Samuel M Wilson in *Hispaniola: Caribbean Chiefdoms in the Age of Columbus*
(1990, University of Alabama Press, pp 55-56) the explorer must have based his assumptions

The first Cubans that Columbus encountered were the peaceful and highly-civilised Taínos. They fished. They hunted. They cultivated yucca, maize, and tobacco. They called their home Cubanacan, meaning "the abundantly fertile land". Fearful when they first caught sight of the Spanish explorers, the Taínos were eventually fascinated. They presumed that these new pale-skinned strangers descended from heaven. The Siboney and Guanahatabetes, who also inhabited the island, came to believe the strangers were deities who adopted human form, scouring the northern coast in search of gold.

Columbus christened, on behalf of the Spanish Crown, this discovery Isla Juana, named after Prince Juan of Asturias who was the king's and queen's only son to survive to adulthood. [*see above*] Columbus and his crew remained on the island until the 12th of November.

on the letters he received in the 1470s from cosmographer Paolo dal Pozzo Toscanelli and the travelogues of Sir John Mandeville's journey to the Orient.

Upon their return to Spain, they presented ten Taíno men and wom-
en plus three children to present to the royal court. As Columbus
believed: "...they might learn our tongue, so as to know what there is
in the country and so that when they come back they may be tongues
to the Christians and receive our customs and the things of the faith.
Because I saw and know that this people has no religion...nor are
they idolaters, but very mild and without knowing what evil is, nor
how to kill others, nor how to take them and without arms and so
timorous that from one of our men ten of them fly, although they
do sport with them and ready to believe and knowing that there is a
God in heaven and sure that we have come from heaven."[5]

Columbus never found the endless veins of gold that Marco Polo's
memoirs and native tales promised. He did, however, realise there
was potential in the planting of "white gold"—sugar cane—in this
new land.

Honey Reed

S ugar cane's unrivalled sweetness tantalised Europeans as early
as 320 BC, when Alexander the Great's admiral Nearchus first
tasted the plant in northern India. He described it as a reed which
"gives honey without bees."[6] This sweet grass grows in many varieties throughout Asia. *Saccharum spontaneum, Saccharum barberi,*
and *Saccharum sinese* grow wild in southern Asia. *Saccharum robus-
tum* proliferates in Indonesia. *Saccharum barberi,* and *Saccharum
sinese* are the canes Nearchus possibly sampled and used in early
Indian and Chinese sugar production. But it was a hybrid of the

---

5   Hale, 56

6   *The Penny Cyclopaedia Of The Society For The Diffusion Of Useful Knowledge* (Charles
Knight, 22, Ludgate Street, and 13, Pall-Mall East 1833). 226

Saccharum officinarum from Papua New Guinea bred with the wild Asian *Saccharum barberi* that was cultivated by the Saracen-Moors (aka: Muslims), later called *Saccharum commune* [*see left*]. They did a strong trade with Europe for the sweet harvests that eventually its way to Hispañola and Cuba.[7]

It was an important commodity for Arab, Venetian, and Genoese merchants. The Saracen-Moor invasion of Sicily, Spain, and Portugal during the eighth and ninth centuries introduced the successful cultivation of sugar cane. Demand was so great by the early fifteenth century that Prince Henry the Navigator of Portugal planted sugar cane on the island of Madeira. Then, by 1483, the Spanish joined in this new enterprise, establishing sugar cane plantations on the Canary Islands.

The young Christopher Columbus began his apprenticeship, in 1473, as a business agent for the Genoese trading consortium of Centurione, Di Negro, and Spinola. Sugar was one of this syndicate's most lucrative commodities. Traveling from the Mediterranean to northern Europe, Columbus learnt the financial value of sugar. Eventually he moved to island of Madeira and then the island of Porto Santo, where he married Filipa Moniz Perestrello, daughter of the governor Bartolomeu Perestrello, a Portuguese nobleman of Genoese birth. [*see opposite*][8]

---

7   J.H. Galloway, *The Sugar Cane Industry: An Historical Geography From Its Origins To 1914* (1st edn, Cambridge University Press 2005) 11; Henry G Dalton, *The History Of British Guiana* (Longman, Brown, Green, and Longmans 1855) 174

8   Janice W Randle, *Issues In The Spanish-Speaking World* (1st edn, Greenwood Press 2003). 46-47

Madeira was already regarded as a major sugar production centre. The island's plantation owners had grown rich from its abundant harvests. After working there for nearly a decade Columbus was well aware of the profit to be had in planting, processing, and trading this sweet, "white gold."

According to Cuban historian Fernando Campoamor, Columbus brought sugar cane seedlings with him, in 1493, on his second voyage to the Caribbean. But there is a sad footnote to this milestone. He was unable to conduct the cultivation experiments he intended to perform on Hispañola (now called the Dominican Republic and Haiti). The delicate plants did not survive the sea crossing. That distinction goes to Pedro di Atienza who, in 1501, successfully planted and harvested sugar cane on the same island. This marked the point at which early settlers discovered sugar cane could flourish in the tropical Caribbean climate.[9]

Blood, Sweat, and Macheteros

Peaceful coexistence was fleeting between the indigenous Cuban people and the Spanish explorers. Columbus's two expeditions to Cuba never developed into the establishment of a settlement.

---

9   F.G. Campoamor, *El Hijo Alegre De La Caña De Azúcar* (1st edn, Editorial Científico-Técnica 1981) 26

In fact, his sole reason for both voyages was to find the fabled land of gold he was certain existed nearby in Japan.

Spanish settlement erupted abruptly and violently on Cuba when conquistadors Diego Velásquez de Cuéllar and his secretary Hernán Cortés [*see left*] arrived, in 1512, with 300 men and boatloads of fresh sugar cane seedlings. These new masters forced the Taínos to clear the lush tropical forest that was their home and then to plant the shoots in the newly-bared earth. The experiment was success.

Seven cities were established on the island in those early days: Baracoa in 1511; Bayamo in 1513; Trinidad, Camagüey, plus Sancti Spiritus in 1514; Santiago de Cuba in 1515; and lastly Havana, which had begun as two separate settlements in 1515 that were united by 1519. Velásquez became the island's governor, Cortés the mayor of Santiago de Cuba. The pair stopped searching for gold, they planted it instead. Within two decades, the Spanish were certain that the legendary El Dorado ["the Golden Man"] and his city resided in South America, where the conquistadors found the palaces, gardens, and people of the Inca Empire gilded in gold.

The majority of the 270 Spanish families who settled in Cuba, by 1570, preferred to concentrate on the relatively guaranteed wealth of sugar cane cultivation and sugar processing. But this wealth did not come without hard investment.

Sugar was a labor-intensive proposition. Land needed to be cleared of its thick vegetation and prepared. Somewhere between 5,000 to 8,000 cane seedlings were planted by hand to produce just one acre of sugar cane. About eighteen months later, mature cane was cut as close to the base as possible—the source of the highest level of sucrose—by *macheteros* [machete wielders] hacking at cane in the thick, sweltering heat.

Then began the complex process of transforming harvested cane into crystallised sugar. Concepción de la Vega on the island of Hispañola was the site for a pioneering breakthrough in sugar production. A resident named Aguilón, around 1506, experimented with rudimentary tools such as the *cunyaya* [*see below*] to extract the *guarapo* [cane juice] from the harvested plants. It took incredible physical strength to operate this simple device and even more power to employ the *trapiche* [sugar grinder] that eventually replaced it. The city's mayor Miguel de Ballester, in 1514, then applied this technology and erected a small commercial sugar mill to supply the local market.[10]

The intense stench of rotting cane and the unbearable heat from the boiling kettles of *guarapo* were beyond human endurance. Workers were rotated in four-hour shifts to crush the cane, to boil the juice, to skim the hot liquid, to transfer it from kettle to kettle thereby reducing the thickening syrup into crystals, and to maintain the fire that was at the heart of the entire process.

At first, the Taínos were forced into labour and housed in squalid conditions. Disease, especially tuberculosis, was surreptitiously imported by Columbus's crew, killing even more labourers than the

---

10   Pieter C Emmer, *New Societies: The Caribbean In The Long Sixteenth Century* (1st edn, UNESCO Publ [ua] 1999) 67

backbreaking work and physical abuse they suffered at the hands of the plantation and sugar mill owners [*see above and opposite*].[11] Smallpox and scarlet soon followed with additional foreign settlement.

One man stood in defence of the indigenous Cubans, Fray Bartolomé de las Casas. The first priest to be ordained in the New World, de las Casas arrived in the Caribbean, in 1502, along with his father. He entered the Dominican order eight years later and was then assigned, in 1512, as a missionary to the tormented Taínos. Eyewitness to the genocide of his spiritual flock at the hands of Velàsquez's conquistadors, de las Casas penned an impassioned letter, in 1515, begging King Ferdinand II to end the wholesale slaughter. With encouragement from

---

11   K. Derla, 'Disease-Carrying Europeans May Have Wiped Out Native Americans' (Tech Times, 2017) <http://www.techtimes.com/articles/146875/20160404/disease-carrying-europeans-may-have-wiped-out-native-americans.htm> accessed 10 April 2016

Archbishop Jimenez de Cisneros of Toledo, Ferdinand appointed de las Casas Priest-procurator of the Indies, protector of the Taínos.

But the genocide did not subside. De las Casas returned to Spain four years later to once again plead his case, this time before King Charles I. His mission met with failure. Unable to gain political support, he wrote an inflammatory account, in 1523, of the atrocities which became the basis for his 1542 book *A Brief Account of the Destruction of the Indies:* "The *Spaniards* first assaulted the innocent Sheep, so qualified by the Almighty, as is premention'd, like most cruel Tygers, Wolves and Lions hunger-starv'd, studying nothing, for the space of Forty Years, after their first landing, but the Massacre of these Wretches, whom they have so inhumanely and barbarously butcher'd and harass'd with several kinds of Torments, never

before known, or heard (of which you shall have some account in the following Discourse) that of Three Millions of Persons, which lived in *Hispaniola* itself, there is at present but the inconsiderable remnant of scarce Three Hundred. Nay the Isle of *Cuba*, which extends as far, as *Valledolid* in *Spain* is distant from *Rome*, lies now uncultivated, like a Desert, and intomb'd in its own Ruins.."[12]

De las Casas's pleas and prayers were partially answered, on 29 May 1537, when Pope Paul III issued the papal bull *Sublimis Deus* [the Sublime God], which declared that the indigenous people of the West Indies to be rational beings with souls and that their lives and property should be protected.[13] Five years later, the Church's stand on the subject compelled King Charles I to sign laws, which prohibited enslavement of the indigenous people. Although the first

African slaves were smuggled into the Caribbean, in 1514, it wasn't until these laws were set into motion coupled with the realisation of enormous profits from sugar that full-scale slave trade commenced in the Caribbean.

The chain of events that followed have been inaccurately reported by most European historians over the centuries.

Chattel slavery was practiced on the African continent as part of the economic fabric as the seventh century AD with the Muslim

THE KING OF ASHANTEE AND HIS GUARDS.

12   Bartolomé de las Casas, *A Brief Account Of The Destruction Of The Indies Or, A Faithful NARRATIVE OF THE Horrid And Unexampled Massacres, Butcheries, And All Manner Of Cruelties, That Hell And Malice Could Invent, Committed By The Popish Spanish Party On The Inhabitants Of West-India, TOGETHER With The Devastations Of Several Kingdoms In America By Fire And Sword, For The Space Of Forty And Two Years, From The Time Of Its First Discovery By Them.* (Project Gutenberg 2007).]

13   'Sublimus Dei' (Papalencyclicals.net, 2016) <http://www.papalencyclicals.net/Paul03/p3subli.htm> accessed 29 December 2015

penetration of the Trans-Sahara.[14] But it was the practice of "local slave trade", in which Ashanti chieftains [*see opposite*] with the aid of Angolan mercenaries [*see right*] waged war, captured, and sold rival African tribes-people to gain valuable territory and resources in addition to profit.[15] This lucrative trade expanded beyond its Muslim origins to include European customers, by the 1500s and 1600s, as Brazilian and Caribbean colonists demanded vast quantities of cheap labour.

On many occasions, slaves were traded in exchange for sugar cane distillates. The tribal chieftains already took pleasure from consuming a malted sorghum and millet brew called *burukutu*. This new, high-proof spirit quickly became a favoured commodity. Consequently, a cycle that provided the necessary man-power to produce sugar was funded largely by the exportation of sugar-based spirits such as cachaça and rum in exchange for more slaves.

The sugar industry in the Caribbean colonies exploded. Cuba alone, in 1620, had some fifty full-scale sugar mills. But then the pace came to a near standstill as Spanish politics and economics interceded.

---

14   J. Alexander, 'Islam, Archaeology And Slavery In Africa' (2001) 33 World Archaeology 44-60

15   Henry Louis Gates Jr., 'How To End The Slavery Blame-Game' (Nytimes.com, 2010) <http://www.nytimes.com/2010/04/23/opinion/23gates.html?_r=0> accessed 24 February 2016

Chapter Two

WATER
OF LIFE

New Land, New Spirit

It may have seemed like the Promised Land to early European emigrants. Sapphire skies, turquoise seas, rich soil, a virgin landscape. It was most certainly was a new frontier, brimming with financial potential. The European powers who followed the Spanish to this economic cornucopia during the 1600s saw sugar cane as the source of untold riches.

The monetary paradise that was Cuba was soon outstripped by the sugar plantations that cropped up on Barbados, Jamaica, the French Antilles, and in Brazil. Wine and beer spoiled on the long transatlantic ocean voyage. Brandy was far too expensive to import. Colonists resorted to producing their own alcoholic beverages. These settlers were familiar with arrack, a southeast Asian distillate made from sugar cane juice, red rice, or coconut flowers that was imported to Europe by Arab and Genoese merchants as far back as the Crusades.

The technology was already perfected in Europe during the 1300s based on earlier Arab alchemical studies and made accessible to a wide audience thanks to the invention, during the 1400s, Johannes Gutenberg's movable type printing press. Thus, the settlers imported their own distillation equipment and instruction manuals to the New World so they could produce not only their own spirits but essential medicines.

Demand for a non-imported and thus less expensive spirit led to the rapid development of domestic alcohol production in all of the New World colonies. With each step sugar cane [*see opposite*] played a dominant role.

Sugar Brandy Is Born

Spanish settlers in Santiago de Tequila, Mexico succeeded, in 1531, in distilling the juice of the native *Agave tequilana* plant and blending it with sugar cane-based spirit to make *mixto*. According to historian Marcelo Cámara, five Portuguese colonists in Brazil established three sugar mills around the same time: São Jorge dos Erasmos, Madre de Deus, and São João. In addition to sugar processing equipment, the partners—Martim Afonso de Sousa, Pero Lopes de Sousa, Francisco Lobo, Vicente Gonçalves, and Erasmo Sheetz of Antwerp— installed copper alembic stills, in 1533, at São Jorge dos Erasmos to produce an *aguardente de caña* [cane brandy] from *guarapa azeda* [sugar cane wine].[16] (Today, this site is a national monument supervised by the University of São Paulo, since 1958, containing the ruins of Brazil's first cachaça distillery.[17]) Fifty-two

16   M Cámara, *Cachaças: Bebendo E Aprendendo* (1st edn, Mauad Editoria Ltde 2006) 10

17   'Monumento Nacional' (Engenho dos Erasmos) <http://www.engenho.prceu.usp.br/monumentonacional/> accessed 15 May 2016

years later, success was apparent. Brazil boasted 192 established distilleries.[18]

Spanish settlers in Cuba experimented with distilling black treacle (aka: molasses) which is the uncrystallised residue that results from the sugar production process. They succeeded at Guayacan, Cuba, in 1598, and named the spirit *aguardiente de caña* [cane brandy].

The Dutch West India Company, chartered in 1621, [*see opposite*] was largely responsible for the development of the "sugar brandy" industry throughout the Caribbean colonies. Brazil became the world's largest sugar producer and exporter after the company captured northeastern Brazil, in 1630, and held jurisdiction over the territory until, in 1654, it capitulated to the Portuguese Crown.

The British settled, in 1627, on the island of Barbados. According to some historical sources, in 1637, Dutch émigré Pieter Blower imported cane seedlings and distillery equipment to the new British colony from Brazil, encouraging the distillation of molasses to extend the value of the sugar cane harvests.[19] A traveler to the island Henry Colt noted that Barbadians were "devourers upp of hott waters [sic] and such named good distillers thereof."[20]

French settlers, on 15 September 1635, landed on the island of Martinique to colonise the territory under the banner of the Compagnie des Îles de l'Amérique which was chartered by Cardinal Richelieu and led by Pierre Bélain d'Esnambuc.[21] However, the sugar and distilling industries were absent until 1644, when the Dutch Jewish

18   Cámara, 12

19   Cámara, 12

20   Vincent T Harlow, *Colonising Expeditions To The West Indies And Guiana, 1623-1667* (1st edn, Printed for the Hakluyt Society 1925) 65. According to Frederick H Smith, Colt's use of the term "good distillers" was employed to imply the heavy drinking habits of the Barbadian settlers.

21   Charles de Rochefort and Raymond Breton, *Histoire Naturelle Et Morale Des Iles Antilles De L'amerique* (Chez A Leers 1658) 40

émigré Benjamin Da Costa introduced sugar processing and possibly distillation equipment from Brazil, following in Blower's footsteps.[22]

Cuban planters also experimented with sugar distillates. Author Miguel Bonera Miranda uncovered an early mention of Cuban *aguardiente de caña* distillation, dating from 1643, in which alderman Álvaro de Luces stated in a meeting that: "in almost all the sugar mills they make *aguardiente de cachaza* and in others *aguardiente de caña* ...which they sell in their bars."[23]

The North American mainland was another landmass that was ripe for settlement and the establishment of a new industry. Escaping both religious and political persecution in their homeland, Brownist English Dissenters (aka: the Pilgrim Fathers) arrived at Cape Cod, Massachusetts, in 1620, on board the Mayflower. The Dutch settled the portions in between, stretching from what is now Connecticut to Delaware, including the establishment, in 1624, of the New Netherlands colony. Further south, the Virginia colony at Jamestown, which was established in 1607, thrived thanks to the successful planting of tobacco as a cash crop. But the Plymouth and New Netherlands colonies had to search for alternative means of economic survival because of the brutally harsh winters and less fertile soil. Fur trading, lumber, pitch, and eventually rum became the most profitable export trade.

Dutch settlers were the first to establish a distillery in these new colonies. Willem Kieft [*see right*] opened his distillery, in 1640, on the island of New Netherlands (now Staten Island) making

---

22   Frederick H Smith, *Caribbean Rum* (1st edn, University Press of Florida 2005) 14

23   Miguel Bonera Miranda, *Oro Blanco* (Lugus 2000) 11

"brandy-wine" from, fruit, molasses, and grain.[24] Emmanuel Downing opened his operation, in 1648, in Salem, Massachusetts. In a letter to Governor John Winthrop, Downing wrote: "The water I make is desired more and rather than the best spirits they bring from London."[25] Winthrop's cousin George Downing had spent five months in Barbados, in 1645, which triggered interest in trade with the island for both molasses and slaves. The Rhode Island colony also successfully established, in 1684, a rum distillery, thus enjoying the profit-making potential that assured the financial success.[26]

Cuba benefited most from the establishment of these northern distilleries. Here were eager, potential purchasers for the island's bounty of molasses, the cheap by-product of the sugar production process. Shipping molasses was also inexpensive because of the island's proximity to the New England and New Amsterdam colonies.

By the turn of the century, Spanish Caribbean rum production threatened southern Europe's grape-spirit industry as exports trickled across the Atlantic. The Spanish crown outlawed rum-making in the Caribbean colonies. Distillers merely went underground with their lucrative operations.

---

24   F.P. Pacult, *American Still Life: The Jim Beam Story And The Making Of The World's #1 Bourbon* (J Wiley 2011). 7

25   Bernard Bailyn, *The New England Merchants In The Seventeenth Century* (1st edn, Harvard University Press 1955) 74

26   F.H. Smith, 'Volatile Spirits: The Historical Archaeology Of Alcohol And Drinking In The Caribbean' (PhD, University of Florida 2001). 63

French Caribbean rum production was also outlawed. But these distillers established a sales network along the Atlantic that avoided metropolitan port cities.[27] French producers such as Joseph François Charpentier de Cossigny differentiated styles by calling the *vesou* [pure sugar cane juice] distillate *guildive* and the spirit made from sugar scum or molasses, *tafia*. *Guildive* was considered the preferred spirit because it was less likely to have an acidic palate.[28]

British Caribbean rum producers fared best of all as the British crown saw this new enterprise as a viable way to attack Spanish and French wine and brandy exportation. Then wars assured the grape industry's declined. The War of Spanish Succession (1701-1714) struck the first blows to wine exportation. Then the Spanish crown ordered that all rum-making equipment be destroyed in its colonies to prevent further decline and encourage Peruvian vineyard production. A decree was issued, in 1739, giving Cuban rum distillers fifteen days to cease operations or face financial and material ruin.[29] Yet the distillers continued to produce their spirit until strict enforcement, in 1754, led illegal distillers to be forced to work on public works without pay until they were impoverished.

The Seven Years War (1756-1763) cut off all trade with the Americas as Britain, French, and Spanish fought for supremacy in the age of empire-building. But it also freed Cuban distillers from Spanish oppression. British forces captured and occupied Havana, in 1762, [*see opposite*] lifting the prohibition on distillation and introducing new equipment and production techniques. Four thousand slaves were imported during this brief occupation, indicating the British

27   Smith, *Caribbean Rum*, pp 55-56

28   J.F. Charpentier de Cossigny, *Mémoire Sur La Fabrication Des Eaux-De-Vie De Sucre Et Particulièrement Sur Celle De La Guildive At Du Tafia; Avec Un Appendice Sur Le Vin De Cannes Et Des Observations Sur La Fabrication Du Sucre* (l'Imprimerie Royale 1781) 1-2.

29   José Chez Checo, El Ron En La Historia Dominicana (Centenario de Brugal 1998) 62-63

intention to exploit Cuba's potential as a sugar colony. After the British occupation, in 1764, Spanish officials found it impossible to control illegal rum production and thus finally lifted the ban.[30]

Revolutions and Evolution

The American Revolution (1765-1783) led to the first rise of the Cuban rum industry. Heavy taxation by the British government on sugar and molasses imports to the colonies stifled the highly-profitable New England and Mid-Atlantic rum industries.

Cut off from Barbadian and Jamaican molasses and rum, American colonists turned their sights to another source. Cuban rum exports rose from less than 50,000 gallons in 1778 to nearly 150,000 gallons in 1781 and 1782, with molasses exports followed an equal

30　Smith, *Caribbean Rum*, pp 55-56

RUM

BY ANY

OTHER NAME

Speculation envelopes the origins of the word "rum". Some people have said the term is derived from the word "rummage". But that word actually dates back to 1582 and implies that a person is making a thorough search of something or some place. Others have said the word descends from the British word "rummer"—or German roemer—which is a type of wine glass. But these vessels appeared in Europe at the same time as the cane-juice liquor, not beforehand.

There is one romantic suggestion that the term "rum" is an abbreviated version of "rumney", a type of sweet wine made in Greece and the southern Balkans that was very popular during the 1400s and 1500s in England.

According to nineteenth-century philologist Walter William Skeat, the term is an Anglicised version of the Malay word "brum", which is an arrack made from sugar cane juice. Historian Frederick H. Smith found that the first documented use of the word "rum" appears in a plantation deed recorded in Barbados in 1650, which identifies the Three Houses estate in St. Philip parish as having "four large mastick cisterns for liquor for Rum."

A year later, Barbardos resident Giles Silvester made the only known reference linking the words "rum" and "rumbullion" when he wrote: "the chiefe fudling they make in the lland is Rumbullions, also Kill Divill, and this is made of Suggar cones distilled in a hott hellish and terrible liquor." The term "rumbullion" was a common word in Devonshire, England that means "a great tumult."

However, its birth came about, the word "rum" was adopted during the 1600s throughout the Caribbean colonies. First appearing in the 1750s in Diderot and Alembert's Encyclopedie, the word "rhum" with an "h" is specifically employed to describe rums made in French colonies such as Martinique and Guadeloupe. The word "ron", indicates the sugar cane liquor was produced in Spanish colonies, the most famous of which is the island of Cuba.

pattern as the American taste for rum and domestic made with Cuban molasses hit an all time high.[31]

It took a revolution on the neighbouring island of Hispañola for Cuban rum to emerge as a driving economic force. The Haitian Revolution on the island's French-colonised Saint-Domingue section begun with a slave rebellion instigated in 1790 by Vincent Ogé and

concluded with the 1801 inauguration of rebel leader François-Dominique Toussaint L'Ouverture [*see left*] as the new nation's Governor-General. The revolution resulted in a mass exodus of French sugar plantation owners who had established a profitable sugar industry on what was France's largest and most profitable colony.[32]

But it wasn't just French planters and their families who fled to Cuba. While studying agricultural methods in Jamaica, in 1794, the Count of Casa Montalvo persuaded French agricultural specialists who had also fled Sainte-Domingue and taken refuge in the British Caribbean colony to join him in Cuba.[33] Thus, scientific knowledge and the potential for progress and improvement also migrated. [*see right, vessels entering Havana harbour*]

The Haitian Revolution had another affect. It not only temporarily stifled the very lucrative slave trade from Africa to the Caribbean. It redirected government interest in Cuba to increase the labour force through the hiring of white immigrants. The potential for slave

31   Smith, *Caribbean Rum* 60-61

32   Smith, *Caribbean Rum* 214-215

33   William R. Lux, 'French Colonization In Cuba, 1791-1809' (1972) 29 Americas (Washington, 1944)

upheaval in Cuba had been voiced since the 1740s and the Haitian Revolution made that threat readily apparent as well as imminent.[34] Thus, the Sociedad Económica de Amigos del País was established, in part, to encourage the substitution of white migrants for African slaves in Cuban labour force.[35]

The new governor of Cuba, Don Salvador de Muro y Salazar, in 1799, then granted land along the coast for the settlement of white refugees from Sainte-Domingue at Nipe, Holguín, Sagra de Tánamo, and Mayarí.

The population of Cuba almost doubled during this decade of migration. The census that was ordered, in 1791, by Governor Luís de las Casas estimated there were about 270,000 adult inhabitants of all races.[36] That figure lurched, in 1804, to 432,080 adults: an increase of 161 percent.[37] Cuba's adult white population on its own surged from a pre-1791 figure of 133,559 to 234,000: a 175.3 percent increase in a little over a decade aided by the addition of French refugees from Louisiana, who arrived after the sale, in 1803, of the French-held Louisiana Territory to the United States.[38]

34   Lux 29

35   Lux 29

36   Lux, 57. However, Willis F.Johnson in *The History of Cuba*, vol II (1920), p 279, notes that this census was possibly inaccurate based on the 1804 assessment made by visiting scientist Baron Humboldt, who estimated the population was closer to 362,000 adults.

37   Lux 58

38   Lux 59

The decline of the sugar and rum industries thanks to the revolution led to an almost immediate upswing in Cuban *aguardiente de caña* exports from 178,000 gallons in 1790 to an 1804 record of 1.6 million gallons.

This transformation was further aided, in 1796, when the Spanish crown lifted the draconian taxation on Cuban *aguardiente de caña*, which was imposed to protect the importation of Spanish spirits to the Caribbean after the repeal of the production ban. This reversal of government policy toward rum making included a crown mandate that required each Cuban sugar refinery owner to install a distillery enterprise. The largest island in the Caribbean—roughly half the size of Great Britain—was poised to become the largest sugar producer in the world and do so with incredible speed.

The change was not only seen in the countryside, but in Havana. What had been a small colonial outpost morphed, in the 1820s, into a grand city. The plantocracy—the governing body comprised of plantation owners—[*see opposite*] built grand houses, dined in fine restaurants, and drank at La Piña de Plata (now known as El Floridita).

They didn't swig the rotgut *aguardiente de caña*. They consumed smooth *ron*, a true product of the Industrial Revolution.

The Industrial Revolution and a New Rum Style

The Watt steam engine developed between 1763 and 1775 by Scottish engineer James Watt [*see right*] and English manufacturer Matthew Boulton ushered in the Industrial Revolution. It was a radical improvement over the Newcomen engine because it employed rotary motion and a separate condenser that did not cool the mechanism's piston and cylinder walls, thereby doubling the engine efficiency. And it was one the first innovations embraced by Cuban planters.

The first steam engine of this type employed in sugar production arrived at the Seybabo sugar mill on 11 January 1797 after plantation owner Count de Mopox y Jaruco placed an order with the Fawcett, Preston Engineering Company, Limited.[39]

But it broke down soon after installation.[40] The first successful attempt at implementation occurred later when Juan Madrazo ordered an engine from

---

39   Manuel Ramón Moreno Fraginals, *The Sugarmill* (1st edn, Monthly Review Press 1976) 102. The firm Fawcett, Preston Engineering, was founded in 1758, by George Perry, as the Liverpool branch of the Coalbrookdale Foundry. It became an independent company and built an international reputation, particularly for sugar machinery.

40   J. M. de la Portilla and Marco Ceccarelli, *History Of Machines For Heritage And Engineering Development* (Springer 2011) 210-211.

FAWCETT, PRESTON & CO., LTD.,
Telegrams—Fawcett, Liverpool.   Codes used—A B C (4th and 5th Edns.), A 1, and Western Union.   **Engineers, LIVERPOOL.**

HEAVY
AND OTHER

CANE-GRINDING PLANTS
and all other classes of
SUGAR MACHINERY.

Also
Sea Water Distilling
Apparatus,
Hydraulic Presses
for baling
cotton, jute, fodder, &c.
&c. &c.
Nitrate-making Plant.

London Office
69, Victoria Street,
S.W.   U1894

ENGINE AND STEEL GEARING for Driving an ELEVEN ROLLER GRINDING PLANT.

Fawcett, Preston [*see above*] in December 1816 and installed it in his sugar mill in Matanzas.[41] Joaquín Peréz de Urria, the Penalver family, and Pedro Diago of the Santa Elena plantation followed suit.[42] (It was not the first application of steam power found on the island. That honour goes to a sawmill in Havana that, in 1810, ordered and installed a Fawcett, Preston steam engine.[43])

Following the lead of Madrazo, de Urria, Penalver, and Diago, other Cuban planters installed 286 steam engines over the next eighteen years. That number soared 336 percent to 961 mills over the ensuing two decades, which meant the vast majority of sugar cane was processed using steam-driven machinery.

---

41   Fraginals 102

42   It is often cited that Diago was the first to install a steam-powered grinder on the island and that it failed to operate. However, records found in the archives of Fawcett, Preston point to four orders being placed and shipped between 1817 and 1818. See also Portunondo, Maria M (2003) "Plantation Factories: Science and Technology in Late-Eighteenth-Century Cuba" in *Technology and Culture* 44:2, 245 and 251

43   Fraginals 102

The Watt engine led in turn to the creation, in 1804, of the steam lo-
comotive by British designers Richard Trevithick and Andrew Viv-
ian. Cuban sugar producers readily adopted this efficient replace-
ment for horse-driven or sail transport of their sugar and molasses
cargoes. Constructed between 1834 and 1837, Cuba's first railroad
solved the problem of transporting sugar and molasses from inland
plantations to the port of Havana. It was also the first rail system
established in Latin America. Within another 23 years, 400 miles
of tracks wove throughout the island. By comparison, Spain did not
see its first railway until 1848 when the Barcelona-Mataró was com-
pleted.[44]

A continuous still [*see right*], designed in 1808 and patented in 1813
by French engineer Jean-Baptiste
Cellier-Blumenthal, afforded planters an opportunity to not only increase production volumes but to
distill a liquid with a lighter character in a single distillation..[45] With
a minor improvement that allowed
for slight interruptions in the continuous nature of the distillation
stream by engineer Charles Derosne,
Blumenthal's device increased its
efficiency by reducing the amount
of heat required to achieve optimum output. The continuous still
evolved even further with design

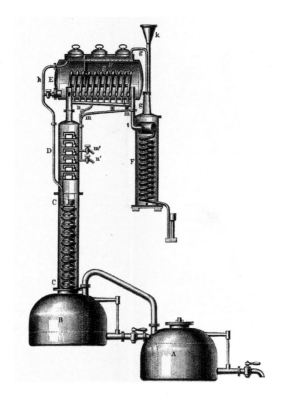

44   'Spain And Portugal' (Railwaywondersoftheworld.com, 2016) <http://www.railway-
wondersoftheworld.com/spain-portugal.html> accessed 1 April 2016.

45   Smith, 214-215; Andrew Ure and Andrew Ure, *Recent Improvements In Arts, Manufactures, And Mines* (1st edn, Longman, Brown, Green, and Longmans 1844) 237

improvements instigated by Sir Anthony Perrier in 1822, by Robert Stein in 1827, and finally in 1831 by Aeneas Coffey. High-volume, fast-output stills were standard by the 1850s in most Cuban rum distilleries.

Technology was not the only factor that played a role in the development of Cuban rum. German chemist Johann Tobias Lowitz (1757-1804) [*see left*] discovered and recorded, in 1785, that charcoal adsorbed noxious odours from sick people, putrid meats, and rotting vegetables. He also found that the substance was excellent for removing the colour from liquids, particularly crystalline acetic acid.[46]

His experiments resulted in the revelation that honey could be made into a pure sugar by boiling it with powdered charcoal. Merely shaking corn-based spirit with powdered charcoal removed fusel oils and unpleasant esters, improving the liquor's aroma and taste. Undesirable colour was quickly whisked away, producing a cleaner form of ethanol. Not willing to stop there, Lowitz tested charcoals made from a variety of woods and recorded which served the best results for the desired purpose.[47]

Lowitz accepted a post in St Petersburg, Russia, in 1793, as Professor of Chemistry at the St Petersburg Academy of Sciences. But this did not stifle his obsession with the transformative effects of charcoal. Within three years, he successfully collected pure ethanol by filtering distillate through hardwood charcoal that was activated to increase its adsorption of undesirable particles and aromas.

---

46   C.R. Noller, *Textbook Of Organic Chemistry* (1st edn, Saunders 1951) 2

47   R.B. Gupta and A. Demirbas, *Gasoline, Diesel, And Ethanol Biofuels From Grasses And Plants* (1st edn, Cambridge University Press 2010) 74

Lowitz's work caught the eye of Antoine-Alexis Cadet De Vaux who, in 1794, detailed his formula for cleaning treacle (aka: molasses) of any unpleasant orders in the publication *Feuille du Cultivateur,* which was subsequently reported by other scientific journals such as the 1794 edition of *The New Annual Register or General Repository of History, Politics, and Literature for the Year 1794.*[48] The process suggested boiling 24 pounds of treacle with 24 pounds of water, and 6 pounds of "thoroughly burnt" charcoal. When the water evaporated, it was noted that: "There is little or no loss by this operation, as twenty-four pounds of treacle give nearly the same quantity of syrup."[49]

French botanist Benjamin Delessert [*see right*] also applied Lowitz's charcoal process, in 1805, to the production of sugar from sugar beets to improve its appearance and aroma. Napoléon Bonaparte awarded him a Legion of Honour for his efforts.[50] Next, French chemist Charles Derosne designed a filtration system that employed bone-based, activated charcoal to filter impurities out of cane syrup. His company, founded in 1812, was the first to enlist this device in the manufacture of beet sugar. Derosne partnered with boilermaker Jean-François Cail, in 1836, to build a dedicated factory to produce his inventions.

48   A.A. Cadet de Vaux, 'Observations Sur Une Matière Sucrée, Suppléant Le Sucre. Procédes À Employer Pour S'en Servir' [1794] Feuille du Cultivateur 79

49   G. Robinson and others, 'Process To Deprive Treacle Of Its Disagreeable Taste, And To Render It Capable Of Being Employed For Many Purposes, Instead Of Sugar' [1794] *The New annual register, or General repository of history, politics, and literature, for the year 1794* 158

50   E. Ponce Lopez, 'The Beet And Napoleon' (2011) 29 *Idesia*. 151-156

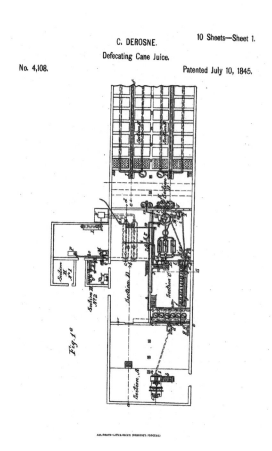

C. DEROSNE.

Defecating Cane Juice.

No. 4,108.

10 Sheets—Sheet 1.

Patented July 10, 1845.

Cuba was an early adopter of Derosne's filtration system [*see left*]. Cuban sugar planters Joaquín de Arrieta, Wenceslao de Villaurrutia, and Pedro Lefranc Arrieta acted as Derosne's agents, setting up the first filtration system, in 1841, at La Mella plantation which was owned by Wanceslao de Urrutia. This device streamlined tasks executed normally by slave labourers. Three years later, both Derosne and Cail recognised that the new filtration system needed to be operated by a skilled sugar master.

Derosne himself travelled to Cuba to train Villaurrutia's machinists and supervise installation on other Cuban plantations, including La Gran Azucarera (San Martino and Santa Susana) and the plantations of the Zulueta family (Habana, Vizcaya and Alava), whose Vizcaya distillation operations were later purchased by the Arechabala family.[51] (The year before his death, in 1846, Derosne finally patented his charcoal filtration device in the USA and assigned the rights to Patent #4,108 to Joseph F. Lapéra.[52])

51   D. Pretel and N. Fernández de Pinedo, 'Technology Transfer And Expert Migration In Nineteenth-Century Cuba' (2013) MWP 2013 UI Working Paper 8-9. The Vizcaya plantation name was later given to the Vizcaya distillery, in 1878, when José Arechabala Aldama purchased distillation equipment from the heirs of Joaquín de Zulueta.

52   'Patent   #:   US000004108'   (Pdfpiw.uspto.gov)   <http://pdf-piw.uspto.gov/.piw?PageNum=0&docid=00004108&IDKey=EE05C7AC-22CC%0D%0A&HomeUrl=http%3A%2F%2Fpatft.uspto.gov%2Fnetahtml%2FPTO%2F-patimg.htm> accessed 16 March 2016.

Not all innovations were imported from outside sources. Caribbean rums, by the early 1800s, were mostly distilled on the same style of copper alembic that require double distillation to achieve a smooth spirit. Cuban planter Fernando di Arritola radically improved the design of his own still, in 1820, adding a coil to the swan-neck conical head. As Fernando Campoamor commented: "de Arritola, using an alembic of his own invention, succeeded in producing a rum superior to its crude Caribbean competitors."[53]

The thought of ageing the rum inspired Pedro Diago to store a few small bottles of rum in "mud-glazed pots" and buried them: one of the earliest attempts at ageing the spirit. However, there were some technical difficulties that could not be readily addressed at that point such as how to control bacterial infection of the liquid due to high humidity.[54] Later oak barrels, acquired from import shipments of wine and flour, were determined to further improve the spirit's character.[55]

The *cuadro estadístico de la Siempre Fiel Isla de Cuba* reported, in 1827, that there were approximately 300 rum distilleries in operation on the island, just as French-Caribbean distilleries went into severe decline partially because their style of rum fell did not appeal to consumers when compared to Cuban ron.[56]

Progress was followed by a bizarre turn of fate. A pair of catastrophic events enveloped Europe's wine-producing nations. A species of fungus that was native to the United States known as *Oïdium tucker*

---

53   Campoamor 83

54   Campoamor ibid.

55   Smith 211

56   Campoamor 64

(aka: powdery mildew) decimated vineyards in France, Spain, Portugal, and Italy as well as the island of Madeira.[57] The *Oïdium* [*see left*] was first noticed by a Mr. Tucker, a gardener in Margate, England, who sent a sample for identification and was credited with its discovery. It was then found on vines at the Palace of Versailles in France, in 1846, where gardeners were able to control its spread with a spray of boiled lime and sulphur. But the same treatment could not be replicated on a large scale and thus spread throughout France to Algeria, Spain, Portugal, Spain, Italy, Switzerland, Hungary, Greece, and Turkey.[58]

The *Oïdium* infection probably originated as European viticulturists, horticulturists, and botanists became increasingly fascinated in the grafting, hybridising, and cultivating vines with North American stock to improve yield and wine quality.[59] Those experiments triggered tragedy.

French wine production alone declined, by 1854, from over 1 billion gallons to only 290 million gallons or less than one-third of its normal output. The source seems to point to the black rot and *Oïdium* blights triggered throughout the United States due to a climatic shift that only offered three years of dry weather conditions that

57   Thomas Pinney, *A History Of Wine In America From The Beginnings To Prohibition* (1st edn, University of California Press 1989) 171

58   P. T. H Unwin, *Wine And The Vine* (1st edn, Routledge 1996) 282

59   H.W. Paul, Science, Vine And Wine In Modern France (1st edn, Cambridge University Press 2002) 18

inhibited the blossoming of infections and infestations in 1853, 1858, and 1859.[60]

Steam-powered trains and steam-powered, ocean-going vessels were faulted by irate growers throughout the continent as being the carriers of this "American disease". And as *Oïdium*-resistant American vines were introduced as a method for controlling outbreaks, an aphid known as the *phylloxera* [*see below*] was inadvertently introduced on the same stock, during the 1860s, once again destroying European vineyards in its wake. It hit especially hard in France.[61] The recovering French wine industry collapsed from 2.2 billion gallons in 1875 to only 618 million gallons in 1889.[62]

Both the *Oïdium* and *phylloxera* blights turned the tide on rum trade between the Caribbean and France. To replenish the alcohol supplies lost to *Oïdium*, in 1854, Napoleon III suspended duties on French Caribbean rum imports. Thus, the French domestic public acquired a taste for rhum. The country imported, between 1854 and 1857, more than one million gallons of rhum alone.[63] As the *Oïdium* crisis subsided so did rhum imports, falling to about 200,000 gallons per year.

But as the *phylloxera* blight swept Europe and once again led to the near ruin of the wine and brandy industry, rum imports jumped by the 1880s to more than four million gallons. At the height of the *phylloxera* crisis, in 1896, France

60   Pinney 171 ; D Kervégant, *Rhums Et Eaux-De-Vie De Canne* (1st edn, Editions du Golfe 1946) 24-25, 485; Unwin 282-284

61   Smith, 211

62   Smith, 211

63   Kervégant 24-25, 485

imported more than 6.3 million gallons of rum. Most of the imported product was rhum from Martinique which shipped about 4.5
million gallons.[64]"

What did this mean for Cuban rum?

As *Oïdium* reached its peak of devastation, in 1854, two important economic events occurred. Even though Britain served as the
global police force that was self-assigned to blockading slave trade
since the Abolition of the Slave Trade Act of 1807 was introduced
by Parliament, the growing empire also opened its ports to foreign
produce, including commodities such as rum which were produced
in slave-holding regions. Cuban rum exports took a major leap that
year, averaging nearly three million gallons per annum. To further
stimulate a growing global economy, Britain equalised foreign rum
import duties, in 1860, putting Cuban rum makers on par with their

British Caribbean counterparts.[65] The following year, France also
reduced import duties on foreign rum to further ease rapidly declin-
ing domestic alcohol supplies.[66]

The importance and profitability of Cuban rum production experienced a seemingly overnight transformation based on a number of
events. First, American sugar syndicates established in Cuba had a
positive impact on both sugar and rum production, especially with
the inception of the Civil War in the United States (1861-1865). Cuban rum exports reached record levels, by 1864, of more than 4.5
million gallons. Although export statistics are incomplete for the
second half of the nineteenth century, it appears that Cuban rum
exports remained high during the European *phylloxera* blight.

---

64   Kervégant 485-488

65   R.W. Beachey, *British West Indies Sugar* (1st edn, Blackwell 1957) 74

66   Kervégant 485

Second, the Franco-Prussian War (1870-1871) may have also contributed to the rise in Cuban exports.[67] Following the military tradition of alcohol rationing in many European nations during this period, rum instead of brandy was sent to French troops who served in the Crimea.[68]

Third, rum was added to the list of alcoholic beverages found on café menus throughout France. Alcohol consumption in Paris, in 1865 alone, totalled per capita at 59 gallons of wine, 21 gallons of beer, and 3 gallons of spirits.[69] The rise in popularity of the workers' cafés [see above] not only in Paris but throughout France, reflected the aspirations of this growing class compiled with the effects of domestic and global economic crises on the cost of social drinking.[70] This was the era in which wine prices rose to 20-25 centimes per glass as supply outweighed demand. By comparison, absinthe, rum, kirsch, and other spirits could be had for as little as 10 centimes outside of Paris as demand dictated an exponentially increasing supply. This afforded the working class a modicum of imagined equality with the hedonistic urban bourgeoisie of the Belle Époque who celebrated café life to the extreme.[71]

67   Alain Huetz de Lemps, *Histoire Du Rhum* (1st edn, Desjonquères 2013) 119

68   Manuel Moreno Fraginals, Frank Moya Pons and Stanley L Engerman, Between Slavery And Free Labor: The Spanish-Speaking Caribbean In The Nineteenth Century (Johns Hopkins University Press 1985)

69   W. Scott Haine, The World Of The Paris Café (1st edn, The Johns Hopkins University Press 1999) 96

70   The Long Depression of 1873-1896 which fell across not only France but the world, had been preceded by reparations due to Germany for the Franco-Prussian War (1871-1873)

71   Haine 91

Fourth, the technological and scientific improvements developed during the Industrial Revolution found eager adapters among Cuban planters. Latecomers to the sugar and rum industries, these entrepreneurs readily embraced and even promoted investment in cost- and labour-saving inventions unlike their older Jamaican, Martiniquan, and Barbadian counterparts who found it difficult to justify additional equipment investment.

Cuba boasted, by 1860, the operation of approximately 1,365 rum distilleries. Although rum developed all over the island, the greatest concentration of production centred around Santiago, Havana, and Cardenas. Havana publishing houses printed and distributed volumes of technical knowledge such as Don Juan Lorenzo Casas's 1860 book *El Manual Teórico Práctico para la Elaboración del Aguardiente de Caña* which presented new distillers with the latest improvements in distillation.[72]

New variations were born: dry, straw-coloured Carta Blanca; golden-hued Carta Oro; amber, sweet, and aromatic Ron Palmas; rich, dark Añejo. As these styles developed, between 1860 and 1890, so did the number of Cuban rum brands. Bacardí y Bouteiller made Ron Refino de consumo corriente (1862). Campos Hermanos introduced Ron Matusalem (1872). Bacardí y Cía SC and Dussaq y Cia. produced Ron Carta Blanca and Ron Palmitas (1873). Fandiño Pérez launched Ron Superior (1875). José Bueno y Cia created Ron Blanco y de Color (1876). José Arechabala Aldama launched Ron Viejo Superior (1878). Canals y Cia made Ron Viejo Superior (1880). Rovira y Guillaume crafted Ron Añejo (1880). Crossi Mestre y Cia distilled Ron Crossi y Mestre (1885). JM Parejo introduced Ron Carta Parejo (1887). Trueba Hermanos launched Ron de las Tres Negritas (1888). R Domenech made Ron Superior (1888). Rovira y Guillaume distilled Ron Añejo Vencedor

72   Miranda 58

(1888). And Nicholás Merino distilled Rum Casa Merino (1889).[73] By the turn of the century, the "white gold" known as sugar had evolved from a lucrative profit centre to a glutted global market.

Caribbean colonies and young nations had no other choice for survival than to capitalise on rum production. Although production was temporarily curtailed during both the Ten-Year War and the Spanish-American War, American interests in Cuban sugar and rum did not founder. The new century witnessed a considerable market shift as the syndicates that had initiated relations with Cuba and Puerto Rico in the previous century negotiated preferential trade deals with the USA, making these former colonies the primary suppliers to the American sugar and rum markets. British and French colonies were dealt a crushing financial blow when they were excluded from this proximal and profitable channel.

Cuba exported more than 2.6 million gallons per annum of aguardiente and rum in the two years before Prohibition in the USA took effect. Even with the ban on American alcohol sales throughout the 1920s, rum-runners managed to export Cuban rum to the Florida coast via staging sites on island of Nassau. But distillers diversified their production to make up for the drop in demand for rum. They made denatured alcohol for perfume and medical applications. The Cuban government stepped in and mandated that all motor fuel must contain 25 percent molasses-based ethanol.[74]

Yet Prohibition did little to suppress the popularity and demand for Cuban rum as Americans clamoured on board passenger ships, airplanes, fishing boats, and yachts to quench their thirst for cocktails at the island's burgeoning array of bars as the decade wore on. The year after the ban was lifted, in 1934, the USA imported 211,000 gallons of Cuban rum and about 10,000 gallons of Puerto

---

73   Miranda 88-89

74   Smith 228-229

Rican rum.[75] The scales tilted two years later when Puerto Rico, after having embraced Prohibition and ceased legal rum production from 1918 until 1933, took advantage of its status as an American territory and began producing rum for the American market without the strictures of import excise. Bacardí became the first multinational rum producer, distilling in Cuba, Puerto Rico, and Mexico. The USA imported 2.4 million gallons of duty-free Puerto Rican, in 1940, and a mere 162,130 gallons of Cuban rum.[76]

With the rationing of grain products in both Great Britain and the USA during the Second World War, rum exports from the Caribbean exploded overnight as consumers demanded alternatives to grain-based gin, whiskey, and vodka. When the fighting ceased, rum surpassed all other spirits consumed in the USA, due in part to fighting troops who had acquired a taste for rum whilst fighting in the European, Asian, and African theatres of war. Cuban rum stateside exports, in 1943 alone, exceeded 7 million gallons and showed no signs of decline two years later when Caribbean overtook all imported spirits, including Scot and Irish whiskey.[77]

The balance shifted once again, between 1959 and 1961, when Fidel Castro became Prime Minister of the newly-formed Republic of Cuba and the USA drafted economic sanctions upon the island because of its communist platform.[78] Response to this first American embargo was announced by Fidel Castro on the same day that its imposition on 19 October 1960. The Cuban government nationalised 382 businesses, "including 105 sugar mills, 13 department stores, 18 distilleries, 61 textile factories, eight

---

75   Smith 230

76   Smith ibid.

77   Smith 231

78   Smith 231

railways and all banks, save the Royal Bank of Canada and the Bank of Nova Scotia." [79] Through Resolution No. 6 which was drafted by the Ministry of Foreign Trade on 1 January 1962, the conglomerate known as Empresa Cubana Exportadora e Importadora de Alimentos (aka: ALIMPEX) was formed to manage the production and distribution of imported and exported food and beverages. [80]

With the vital USA market eliminated, distilleries relied upon the very limited market afforded by trade agreements for the purchase of both rum and industrial ethanol with the Union of Soviet Socialist Republics. Global exports of Cuban rum, between 1960 and 1964, totalled only 5.8 million gallons. [81] The increase in both domestic consumption and in the call for industrial ethanol shifted the balance of production. (In fact, Cuba produced, between 1970 and 1987, 230 million gallons of industrial ethanol.) But thanks, in part, to the system of government rum rations and a call for increased production, during the 1970s, Cuban distilleries produced more liquor for its domestic use than for export. [82]

An official visit to Santa Cruz del Norte by Fidel Castro led to the announcement, on 27 February 1971, that the existing, nearly-ruined distillery at that location would be rebuilt and equipped with state-of-the art Austrian stills. The finished building was approved, in 1974,for production. The Havana Club name and visual trademark were filed, on 12 June 1974,

79   Merrill Fabry, 'The U.S. Trade Embargo On Cuba Just Hit 55 Years' [2015] Time <http://time.com/4076438/us-cuba-embargo-1960/> accessed 12 October 2016.

80   'QUIÉNES SOMOS?' (Alimport.com.cu, 2016) <http://www.alimport.com.cu/?page_id=100> accessed 25 October 2016.

81   Junta Central de Planificación, 'Comercio Exterior De Cuba. Exportación' (Junta Central de Planificación 1960) 5, 7-9, 14-15, 26-28

82   Smith 231

with the US Patent and Trademark Office (USPTO), which granted registration certificate #1031651 on 27 January 1976.[83]

The distillery launched, in 1975, its first export, Havana Club Carta Blanca. The success of this revitalisation effort was obvious when Cuban alcoholic beverage exports shot from 1.73 million litres in 1971 to 9.1 million litres in 1976.[84] Foreign and domestic interest these new rum brands was obvious. Four years later, the distilleries produced 40.19 million litres of rum and exporting 15.25 million litres of that output.[85]

Government investment and expansion of the alcohol industry continued to grow both the domestic and foreign markets for both rum and industrial alcohol during the 1980s with dozens of regional companies established to support the demand for what became a high quality, marketable commodity thanks to numerous production studies and improvements.

To further streamline this increased output, Corporation Cuba Ron SA was created by the Ministry of Food Industry on 8 November 1993 to oversee rum production and trade for both domestic and foreign markets. Next, on 10 November 1993, the Havana Club Holding SA was founded to manage the most prestigious brands of Cuban rums. On the very same day, the Council of Ministers of the Republic of Cuba finalised a trade agreement with the French corporation Pernod-Ricard SA for the marketing of Havana Club rums in foreign markets. The timing could not have been more fortuitous.

Revived interest amongst a new generation of young adults in classic cocktails and mixed drinks blossomed, during the 1990s, in both North America and Great Britain. That enthusiasm also embraced

---

83   U.S. trademark registration 1031651 retrieved on 29 October 2016 from http://
tmsearch.uspto.gov/bin/showfield?f=doc&state=4809:k62t08.2.40

84   Miranda, Tomo II, 251-252

85   Miranda, Tomo II, 262

Cuban drinks and their descendants, Tiki drinks. Spreading worldwide, cocktail culture saw rum exports sore by 2000 to 11.69 million litres or 20 percent of the total 59.2 million litres produced.[86]

The success of this joint-venture led to the construction of a new distillery in San José de las Lajas to produce all aged Havana Club rums. It was a major investment that led to the founding of possibly the biggest distillery of aged rums in the world. Cuba's rum exports, in 2015, exceeded 30 million litres, by far the highest figure in the entire history of Cuban rum.

As of this writing, the embargo imposed by the American government on Cuban products is still in effect. However, on 14 October 2016, US President Barack Obama lifted restrictions on American tourists purchasing for personal consumption Cuban cigars and rums outside of the United States. This came on the heels of the Obama administration partially lifting the ban, in January 2015, allowing Americans traveling directly to Cuba to return home with up to $100 in rum and cigars in carry-on luggage.[87]

As you can see, Cuban rum is and has always been revolutionary. Cuban rum always strives to be innovative. Thus, it is no surprise that its arrival coincided with an increased self-awareness amongst its people. Cuban distillers may have been the first to apply the latest scientific methods. But they combined this with a passion for their craft. Cuban rum wasn't born in a laboratory. It sprang from the soil of the island; from the lush harvests of sugar cane; from the souls of a people who forged their own identity and revelled in their culture; from a people who shared the desire for self-determination. In essence, Cuban rum was new because Cuba itself was new, inspired by numerous cultures to create a wholly unique entity. But what makes Cuban rum stand out amongst the world's sugar-based distillates?

---

86   MIranda, Tomo II, 372

87   Alan Gomez, 'Obama Lifts Restrictions On Cuban Rum, Cigars' *USA Today* (2016)

Habana. Corte de Caña
Cutting sugar-cane.

Chapter Three

A LIVING TRADITION

Passion and Art Marry Expertise and Science

It is a revered tradition, a tradition that is very much vital and alive in Cuba. The rum-making process is a symphony of rituals executed a tightly choreographed series of movements, played time and time again by passionate performers before a discerning audience of rum connoisseurs. This is way the fine Cuban rums are made. The opening allegro takes place amid the sights and sounds of harvest time in the lush sugar cane fields that span the length and width of the island of Cuba .

A slow, almost solemn sonata sets the pace for the transformation of fresh sugar cane into juice, juice into molasses, molasses into aguardiente, aguardiente into rum. A rondo of repetitive tasting and ageing steps set out in well-rehearsed score performed by the *maestro del ron cubano* [master blender] who knows what subtleties and digressions must be executed to achieve the desired crescendo of aromas and flavours that are experienced with every sip.

The finale is a lively scherzo in which aged rums are selected and blended into a comprehensive, sensual experience that leaves the audience applauding with a resounding "bravo"!

The performers in this orchestra have taken their places. The conductor has taken up his baton. Let the symphony of rum-making begin.

Thick, green fields of ripe sugar cane sprawl across the landscape as far as the eye can see: from the Sierra Maestra to the Vuelta Abajo, from Santiago de Cuba to Pinar del Rio. It is now December. This is when *zafra* [the sugar cane harvest] begins.

Zafra

The soft rustle of cane leaves swaying in the gentle breeze is punctuated by a whoosh, as machete meets cane stalk. The country hums with the sounds of *macheteros* [cane cutters] wielding their blades, [*see below*] machinery loading fresh-cut bundles, tractors towing overladen trailers. The railways built in the 1800s to transport these precious harvests speed the cane towards the towering brick chimneys of the *ingenios* [sugar mills] that punctuate this tropical rural landscape.

At the heart of all Cuban rums is treacle (aka: molasses, sometimes called "fine honey" or *miel* [honey]) that is obtained from a hybrid sugar cane variety that is cultivated and harvested in Cuba. There are people already hard at work, criss-crossing the countryside, selecting the cane harvests that they need to produce a particular type and style of rum while the cane still stands in the fields.

The island's climate—ranging between 20°C and 35°C for about 320 days per year—is a major contributor to the cultivation of sugar cane that produces a high sugar yield and low water content.[88] The unique winter weather conditions—from November through April—are ideal for harvesting sugar cane, providing low temperatures and lower rainfall than is found in the surrounding geographical region. By contrast, the

---

88   'Ordinary Official Gazette Of The Republic Of Cuba' (Ministry of Justice 2013) 1634-1635

heat and steady rains of summer—from May through October—generate superior growth in the maturing cane.[89]

From Guarapo to Miel

After the cane is cut, the *guarapo* [sugar cane juice] is pressed out of the stalks, boiled again and again until it transforms into crystallised sugar. What remains is a thick, rich, sweet substance that Cuban refiners call molasses, treacle, or *miel*.

This is the basic, raw element from which Cuban rum is made. In fact, during the 1700s and 1800s, Cuban molasses was highly prized by North American rum distillers, who purchased barrels directly from the sugar mills until the launch of Prohibition in the USA.

With relatively low acidity and a high, 55 percent sucrose content, the tradition of Cuban molasses manufacture enjoys a very low sulphur content. This means that when the molasses combines with the natural air-borne microflora during fermentation, it does not retain the "rotten egg" aroma found in other types of molasses which contain a high level of sulphur dioxide.[90]

The *maestro* carefully selects the molasses to be distilled, which is moved via truck or transport car to the *ronera* [distillery]. At its new home, it is then filtered through activated charcoal, sterilised, and diluted with absolutely pure water. Water, in fact, is the second secret of Cuban rum. Because water makes up the greater portion of the rum recipe, its quality is carefully controlled and guaranteed through a series of purifying treatments.

---

89   Ordinary Official Gazette 1634-1635

90   ibid.

The Alchemist's Art

The marriage of molasses and water forms a mixture called *batición* [loosely translated as "shaking"]. Another relationship takes places when this liquid meets yeast. It is not the wild yeast used in some distillations such as cachaça or rhum agricole. Fermentation of this fine mixture is enhanced by a strictly controlled mixed yeast culture of the *Saccharomyces cerevisiae* type, which has been employed by the island's distillers for over 60 years, making it unique from other yeasts of the same style because of its long and intentional isolation.[91]

Placed in huge vats for about 30 hours, the yeast and batición are allowed to naturally ferment under strictly supervised conditions. [*see left*] Microbiologists as well as physio-chemists are on hand to

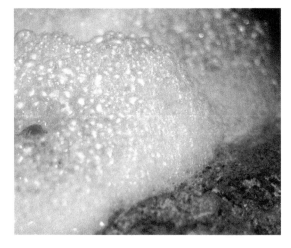

assure that the fermentation stays within a safe range and will yield the desired aromas and flavours that are fundamental to the rum's character.

There are technical specifications for the continuous stills used to distil the fermented "wash" of molasses and water at exact the speed at which vapours travel up the distillation column as well as the amount of time and volume in which the liquid resides on the compulsory copper plates within the still's enrichment area. The distillation plates themselves must be designed to avoid high temperatures that could burn the liquor. Finally,

---

91   Ordinary Official Gazette 1634-1635

fractional condensation is employed to select the precise heart-cut of the distillate that provides the optimum aguardiente for ageing into rum.[92] The *maestro* knows the exact moment to collect this highly desirable portion. He knows precisely when the collection must cease to keep the lingering "tails" from influencing the bouquet of the aguardiente: its aromas and flavours.

The Fortress of Rum

The fragrance of rich oak permeates the humid air in the *ronera's* ageing cellars. Entire ramparts of 180-litre casks rise to impressive heights shored up by bracing. In the heart of these fortresses of rum, it is not unusual to be struck with awe by the vision, by the atmosphere, by the promise of things that will transpire within the casks themselves. This is where the true magic of Cuban rum takes place.

The *ronera's* position is ideally situated: the humidity levels and temperature favour the best of all possible ageing conditions. The island's climate provides a stable and fast-working environment for ageing these rums. (Ageing is considered void if the temperature falls below 15°C. And in fact, by law, ageing houses must maintain and average temperature of 30°C and average lighting conditions throughout the process.)[93]

Everything in the *ronera's* ageing cellars is monitored: the quality and age of the American white oak casks previously used to age bourbon; climate fluctuations that occur during the ageing process; the ventilation of the cellar itself via latticed windows. [*see left*] There will

---

92   Ordinary Official Gazette 1634-1635

93   ibid.

be an "angel's share" that escapes during the ageing process. The heat and humidity of the tropical Cuban climate means a larger portion of angel's share is sacrificed than is found in whisky or cognac production. Nevertheless, it is a small price to pay for the final, ecstatic results.

All Cuban rums must be naturally aged in more than one stage in this carefully monitored environment. Essences, aromas, artificial additives, macerations, extracts, or any chemical of any kind aimed at imitating the ageing process of Cuban rums are prohibited by law. White rums must undergo at least two ageing stages. Dark rums must develop in at least three stages, deriving the maximum compounds from the oak casks in which they are stored. Each ageing stage is preceded by blending aged distillates which regenerates the ageing process and thus improves the overall character.[94]

Añejamiento

In the first stage of ageing, the aguardiente rests for a minimum of eighteen months, enough time to create a *basse oro* [soul], a relationship between the aromas and flavours of both the spirit and the wood.

The rested aguardiente is allowed to pass drop-by-drop through casks that contain various layers of activated charcoal, taking a page from Lowitz's and De Vaux's methods, from the 1790s, for refining molasses. This process removes the sulphur dioxide that can potentially cast a rough profile on the distillate. With the unwanted aromas and flavours eliminated, it is ready it for its next phase of identification and further ageing. The aguardiente is then mixed with *distillado* [pure sugar cane distillate] and water to produce what is called *ron fresco* [young rum]. Then it's aged again.

This is when the art of the *maestro* reaches its peak. Deep in the *ronera's* cellars, he opens each cask, tastes and determines its future. Will it be a blended elaborate, less-aged white rum: a light, warm rum, transparent and as flavourful as fresh sugar cane juice. Will it be a *madre* [mother] who will undergo further *añejamiento* [second-

ary ageing] in previously-used American white oak casks [*see above*] with a capacity of 180-200 litres. This process re-oxygenates the liquid and aids in the removal of tart and sour notes.[95] Thus it is reborn as an *añejo*, the epitome of the Cuban rum spectrum.

An optional third stage is exercised on a select group of *madres* that are destined to become dark, extra-vintage rums. Once again the re-oxygenation revives the ageing process in another round of *añejamiento* in used American white oak casks with a 180- to 200-litre capacity.[96]

The true mark of a *maestro* is to be as humble as the *añejos* he produces, blending rums that have been lovingly set aside by himself and his predecessors. He must be generous with the best batches, setting them to age further so that future rums blended by his successors will be even better. This is an art that cannot be learnt in school or by reading books. It must be personally handed down and nurtured one on one, from one master blender to another.

To start, the *maestro* must recognise each cask in his cellar by sight, just as the shepherd knows each sheep in his flock. His disciple accompanies him, committing to memory the story behind each and every cask.

Constantly refining an organoleptic perception in a mute sensorial dialogue over the years, the *maestro* and his disciple arrive at a perfect symbiosis in their choices of casks as well as the method in which they will be blended. A balance in aromas and flavour coupled with consistency is the ultimate goal.

Backed by a panel of professional tasters who regularly analyse the qualities of each batch of rum, the maestro tastes and does not spit in the fashion well-known amongst vintners. Fine Cuban rum must be swallowed to appreciate its finish. After this tasting, each rum is then chemically and biologically tested to precisely determine potential development of each batch. Each cask has its own distinctive character and possesses a privileged destiny.

After each fixed interval in the añejamiento process, the maestro del ron cubano executes a subtle blending session. The final touch. The *toque* [*see opposite*]. It is a delicate moment, in which the *maestro* puts all of his experience and know-how to the test. Under his orders, the cellar workers roll the barrels before him, open the taps, and allow marvellous streams of the two amber, aromatic liquids run together.

After settling for several weeks, each of these custom blends finds its balance and harmony. The *maestro*'s *añejo* rums now possess distinctive personalities. Does this cask become an aged cocktail rum? Is it a sipping rum? Or is it a special, sensual experience to be enjoyed by true connoisseurs? Does it need more time to achieve its true character? Only the *maestro* knows the heart and soul of each cask, of each blend that he orchestrates in this symphony of aromas and flavours that is real Cuban rum.

The range of aged Cuban rums created by these *maestros* are classified by the percentage of rum that has been in aged in 180-litre oak casks is included in the blend. Each age category is protected by Geographical Designation.

But the artistic process does not end there. Cuban bottlers have an understandable reverence for these prestigious rums that are *hecho en Cuba* [made in Cuba]. Smiling young women with their lively speech and communicative courtesy work quickly and efficiently to smooth a label or check the appearance of each bottle in the *ronera*'s bottling department. Accompanied by a parting burst of good humour: another Cuban rum is ready to enter the world.

There is only one way to know that a bottle of Cuban rum is authentic. Look for the seal of authenticity issued by the Cuban government which must be affixed to each and every bottle that is exported. This guarantee of authenticity is also backed by its Geographical Designation, which is identical to the *Appellation d'Origine Contrôlée* (AOC) granted by the French government to agricultural products, including wine and spirits.[97]

The Republic of Cuba is a signatory of the Lisbon Agreement for the Protection of Designations of Origin and its International Register as well as of the Agreement on Trade-Related Aspects of Intellectual Property Rights (TRIPS), which regulates what can be called authentic Cuban rum. The Corporación Cuba Ron S.A. was granted the right to use the "Cuba" designation only on rums that are produced on the island of Cuba. Since November 1993, the Cuban Ministry of Food Industry has been responsible all rum production, trading, and export as a centralised agency.[98]

---

97   Ordinary Official Gazette 1598-1599

98   ibid.

Besides demonstrating the pride with which these rums are made, this guarantee of authenticity seal that is affixed to each and every bottle assures consumers that the contents is a premium quality, genuine Cuban rum that is produced in Cuba, distilled from Cuban molasses, filtered and aged according to traditional Cuban methods. Accept nothing less.

Points of Difference

As you can now imagine, not all rums are manufactured in the same way. So what are the production differences amongst Cuban or Spanish style rums versus British and French rums?

Climate and terroir vary throughout the Caribbean. The species of sugar cane grown also ranges from island to island. Thus, no rum style is identical to another; each island possesses its own techniques from the planting of the cane to the ageing of the spirit.

French rhum agricoles produced in places such as the islands of Martinique, Haiti, and Guadeloupe share much more in common with Brazilian cachaça than other rum styles. Freshly-crushed sugar cane juice is mixed with cultivated yeast and taken through a batch process of controlled fermentation which takes about three days. The wash is then distilled to 70% abv in either pot or column stills in a single shot, which is then diluted to between 40% and 55% abv. The result is a vegetal spirit with a strong fruit character. Rhum industriel is produced in a similar fashion, using molasses instead of fresh cane juice.

Barbadian rums are generally the lighter of the British-style rums. Molasses wash is fermented for about three days with a cultivated yeast and distilled to 95% abv, using either pot or continuous stills.

Diluted to 68° prior to ageing in small casks for at least one year, the resulting spirit has deep vanilla and fruit notes.

High-ester Jamaican and Guyanese rums are the opposite end of the British spectrum. These molasses-based spirits are generally double distilled: the first distillation occurs below 25% abv and the second distilled to over 70% abv. Dunder—the remains of previous distillation runs—is often added to the wash mixture, giving this particular rum style a distinctive character. Pot stills are the most common equipment used to produce this style, although wooden Savalle and Coffey stills are employed in the making of Guyanese rum. These rums are rich, spicy, fruity, and somewhat heavy.

Although each rum style has its attributes which make them popular in punches or drinks such as the Dark 'n' Stormy, it is the lighter, more accessible character found in the Spanish style, especially Cuban style that has made it more appealing for use in mixed drinks and cocktails and more comparable to Irish whiskey and cognac as a digestif.

Tasting Cuban Rum

Tasting real Cuban rum—just like experiencing fine wine, whisky, or cognac—commands the use of a distinct vocabulary. Like the music in Havana's streets, Cuban rum plays on the palate in major chords rather than single notes. It tantalises the eyes with its range of colours and shades. It delights the nose with its bouquets. It coaxes the palate, inspiring a profusion of descriptive verses from the first sip to the long finish. Once the final notes have been played, Cuban rum can be savoured and enjoyed responsibly in memory for years to come.

There are as many differences amongst rums as there are among whiskeys and whiskies. The quality of the *rons frescos*, the condition of the casks, the temperature of the ageing cellar and the time spent ageing are all variables to be considered in a rum's evaluation. Perceiving these differences is more a matter of training than talent. Here are a few tips from the experts in conducting a proper rum tasting.

The Environment

A proper rum tasting should be conducted in an odour-free, well-lit room that has at least one bright, white surface—a table, a wall, or even a napkin—that can serve as a backdrop for viewing each sample. Participants should not wear heavy perfumes, colognes, or deodorants. Prior to the session, they should not consume any strong flavours such as coffee, garlic, or pungent spices for at least thirty minutes.

Evaluate each rum sample at room temperature (75°-78°F or 23°-25°C). The samples should be served at full strength. Use a standard white wine glass or a specially-designed rum tasting glass [*see right*] that is clean, free of soap residue, and dried with an unbleached drying cloth. Pour approximately 30 ml [1 ounce] of rum into the tasting glass. Then, one-by-one, follow the sensory evaluation steps in the following order: sight, smell, taste, and touch.

Tasting with the Eyes

Hold the glass in front of a bright-white backdrop. Check that your sample is dust-free and particulate-free. Assess the colour. Does the liquid have a silvery cast or a pale golden hue? Is it deep golden or as dark as caramel?

Lightly swirl the rum around the glass. This opens up the aromas by increasing the surface-area-to-volume ratio of the rum in the glass. By doing this, the glycerol content can also be judged. As the rum sinks back into the glass, look for a thick appearance that indicates how the rum will rest on the tongue. Will it be viscous or thin? Glimpse the degree of richness and fullness that you eventually will feel on the palate. Some authorities say that if the rum streams down the sides of the glass in a rosary-bead chain of small drops, it has a higher alcohol level. The bigger the beads, the lighter the spirit content.

Tasting with the Nose

Bring the rim of the glass up just under your nose and open your mouth below the rim. Then inhale only through your nose. This allows the aroma to swirl across the back and top of your palate, where it reaches additional receptors. To experience the difference, try smelling the rum with your mouth closed. You'll soon discover that open- and closed-mouth tasting are radically different. There are subtle aromas that can only be detected when your mouth is open.

Tasting with the Tongue

Just like fine wine, fine rum should be "chewed". Slosh the rum around in your mouth and inhale across it to bring out the full flavours. After the initial "chew", bring the glass back up to your nose to round out the flavour experience. Some purists may balk at this. However, the idea is not to separate taste and smell, but to gain the fullest possible sensory experience. Next, judge the taste three ways: first, on its composition; second, on its intensity; and third, on its duration or finish.

Tasting with the Mouth

Most people tend to forget that this fourth sense is also involved in sensory evaluation. The rum's mouth feel can reveal points of quality which aren't as apparent in its aroma or taste. Warmth versus a burning alcohol feel is a perfect example.

A viscose texture is another. Is the liquid thin and astringent leaving the mouth feeling drier than before you tasted it? Or does it coat the palate?

Now that you know how to properly taste and evaluate real Cuban rum, which ones are available for you to try?

Authentic Cuban Rums to Try

The Cuban rum industry is managed by the government's Cuba Ron Corporation S.A. Under this umbrella only a small selection of rums are sold in Cuba as well as for export. (Other brands are sold only to the Cuban market.) All these brands bear the seal of authenticity of Cuban origin. The following list will give you an idea of what is available for global and limited export markets:

RON ARECHA is produced in Santiago de Cuba: Carta Blanca (38% abv); Carta Oro (38% abv); Añejo (38% abv); Añejo Reserva (38% abv); and Añejo 15 Años (38% abv).

RON CUBAY is produced in Santo Domingo in Villa Clara province: Carta Blanca (38% abv) is aged for 3 years; Añejo (38% abv) is aged for more than 5 years; Carta Dorado (38% abv) is aged for 4 years; Añejo Suave (37.5% abv); Reserva Especial 10 Años (40% abv); and Cubay 1870 (40% abv).

RON EDMUNDO DANTES is produced in Santiago de Cuba: Añejo 15 Años (40% abv) has an annual production limit of 3,000 bottles of rum per year; only 150 bottles of Añejo 25 Años (40% abv) are produced each year exclusively exported for the Spanish market.

RON HAVANA CLUB is produced in two different facilities. Santa Cruz del Norte distills for the Añejo Blanco and Añejo 3 Años. San José de Lajas produces all the other categories. The entire brand portfolio is distributed worldwide in partnership with Pernod-Ricard: Añejo 3 Años (40% abv); Añejo Especial (40% abv); Añejo Reserva (40% abv); Añejo 7 Años (40% abv); Selección de Maestros (45% abv); Añejo 15 Años (40% abv); Tributo (40% abv); Unión (40% abv); Máximo Extra Añejo (40% abv).

RON LEGENDARIO was originally distilled at Fabrica Bocoy in Havana. Today, it is produced in six distilleries in Matanzas, Villa Clara, Havana, as well as three facilities in Pinar del Rio: Carta Blanca Superior (40% abv); Dorado (38% abv); Añejo (40% abv); and Gran Reserva 15 Años (40% abv).

RON MULATA[99] is only 20 years old and produced by Tecnoazucar in Villa Clara: Añejo Blanco; Añejo 5 Años; Añejo 7 Años; and Gran Reserva 15 Años.

RON SANTIAGO DE CUBA is produced in Santiago de Cuba: Carta Blanca (38% abv); Ron Añejo (38% abv); Ron Añejo Superior 11 Años (40% abv); Ron Añejo Superior 12 Años (40% abv); Ron Extra Añejo 20 Años (40% abv); and Ron Extra Añejo 25 Años (40% abv).

RON VARADERO is produced in Santiago de Cuba exclusively for the Italian and Scandinavian import markets: Ron Varadero Silver Dry; Ron Varadero Añejo; Ron Varadero Añejo 3 Años; Ron Varadero Añejo 5 Años; Ron Varadero Añejo 7 Años; and Ron Varadero 15 Años.

The traditions and legends that are associated with real Cuban rum journey far beyond its birth, its growth, and its maturation as a globally-recognised spirit category. Real Cuban rum inspired the birth of as unique mixed drink genre that is its turn begat a style that is equally appreciated on an internal scale. These enduring libations emerged from now iconic bars, crafted by the hands of Cuban cocktails' bartending legends. These people and places are the subject of our next chapter. They created the Golden Age of Cuban Cocktails, an enduring age that cannot be ignored.

---

99   Not to be confused with the rhum agricole distilled in Martinique by the same name.

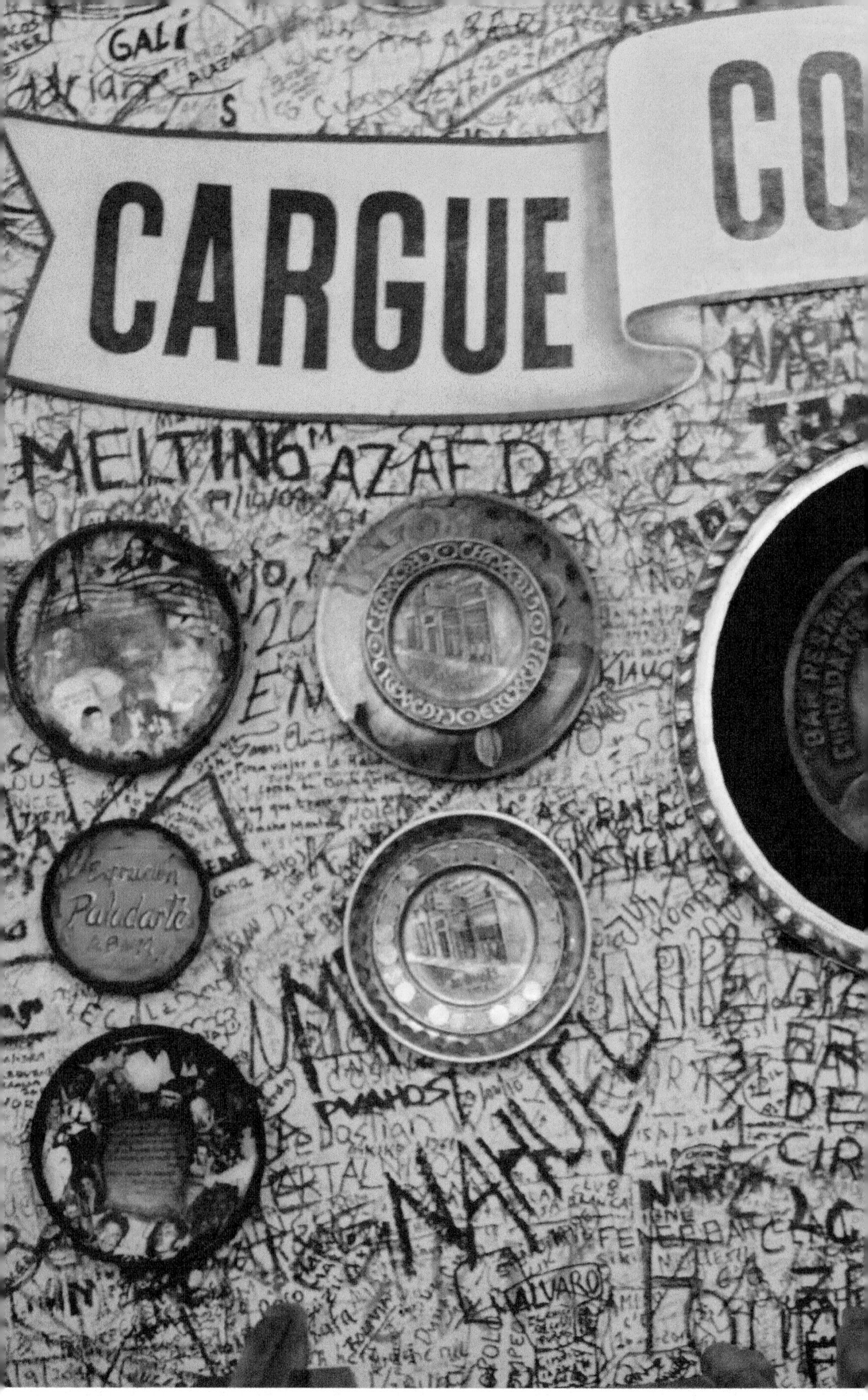
CARGUE

Chapter Four
CLASSIC CUBAN BARS
AND BARTENDERS

Havana at the turn of the twentieth century was known as the "world's loveliest playground."[100] Michel-Claude Touchard defined this Caribbean capital in his 1990 book *L'Aventure du Rhum* as a privileged enclave in which rum brought together the world's most famous actors, best-selling authors, idle heirs, and a variety of personalities that weren't yet called the "jet set". The city's bars, the *cantineros* [bartenders] who presided over them, and even the drinks themselves all have fascinating tales to tell. We begin with the most famous of these establishments—the Cradle of the Daiquirí, El Floridita.

El Floridita

When the *bodega* [cellar] *La Piña de Plata* [The Silver Pineapple] opened in Havana at the corner of Calle Obispo and Monserrate, in 1817, it sold fresh juices served icy cold. In fact, its speciality was fresh pineapple juice. Situated at the head of the busy thoroughfare that leads to Plaza de Armas and the governor's palace, La Piña de Plata served a host of VIPs, politicians, and the city's elite when it opened its doors. Beverage sales were so successful that, in 1867, the establishment installed a restaurant and a bar, then changed its name to La Florida.

The establishment gained an even greater reputation when Don Narciso Sala Parera [*see right*] arrived from Spain and took over ownership, in 1898, changing its name to La Florida. Seemingly overnight, the place was transformed.

---

100   Basil Woon, When It's Cocktail Time In Cuba .. (1st edn, H Liveright 1928) 28

Parera trained his staff to mix their drinks the old fashioned way, the Spanish way, allowing the liquid fall gracefully between two mixing glasses held one high above the other whilst holding back the ice with a julep strainer in the higher of the two glasses [*see opposite*]. It was a technique traditionally employed in northern Spain's *siderías* [cider bars] as well as by European barmen. (Parera even taught his Cuban-born cousin Miguel Boadas the technique when, in 1908, he hired him as a barman.[101])

Another Spanish barman moved, in 1900, with his family to Havana from the Catalan coastal village of Lloret del Mar on northeastern Spain's Costa Brava. He found himself working for Parera. A few years later this proud professional asked his sixteen-year-old son if he wanted to learn the bartender's art. His son, in fact, did. He began working, in 1904, by his father's and Parera's sides. His name was Constantino Ribalaigua Vert. [*see left*]

Accessible, amiable, admirable, customers called him "Constante" [Constant]. British writer Basil Woon observed the choreography surrounding the making of six Mary Pickfords by Constante, in 1927, remarking that: "The drink is shaken by throwing it from one shaker and catching it in another, the liquid forming a half-circle in the air. This juggling feat having been performed several times, Constantino empties the glasses of ice, puts them in a row on the bar, and with one motion fills them all. Each glass is filled exactly to the brim and not a drop is left over."[102]

---

101   Alberto Gomez Font, 'From Chicote To The Kalimocho: A Century Of Cocktails' (2009) 3 *Mixologist: The Journal of the European Cocktail*. Boadas then carried this tradition back with him when he in turn emigrated, in 1925, to Barcelona. Within a few years Boadas opened Bar Boadas, one of the Spain's earliest locations dedicated to serving cocktails.

102   Woon 41

When Parera was ready to retire and return to Spain, in 1918, Constante was in the position to purchase ownership of the now-famous establishment that attracted the attentions of not only Cuba's elite, but the increasing number of American tourists.

No visit to Havana was complete without a cocktail, or two, or three at La Florida: *La Cuna Del Daiquirí* [The Cradle of the Daiquirí]. Although the Daiquirí Natural has its roots in the thirst-quenching Cancháncharra, it was at Bar La Florida that the Daiquirí Frappé (aka: Daiquiri No. 4 or Howard and Mae) evolved and gained worldwide attention even before the venue was rechristened El Floridita.

The establishment's neo-classical criollo décor features columns framing a mural that depicts Old Havana. It has long bar that is staffed with impeccably uniformed bartenders. An elegant dining room in the back offers a more intimate setting. Together the elements make this landmark a regular pit stop for the sophisticated and the fashionable. Its glamorous image was such that *Esquire Magazine* compared it, in its December 1953 issue, to the Hotel Shelbourne in Dublin, the Piped Piper Bar at the Palace Hotel in San Francisco, the Ritz bars in both London and Paris, the Long Bar at Raffles in Singapore, and the 21 Club in New York.[103]

103   Leslie Saalburg, 'World's Seven Greatest Bars' [1959] *Esquire* 175-179

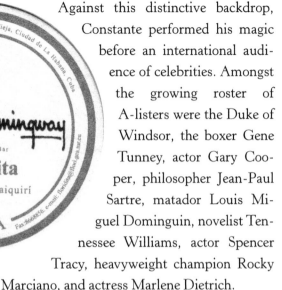

Against this distinctive backdrop, Constante performed his magic before an international audience of celebrities. Amongst the growing roster of A-listers were the Duke of Windsor, the boxer Gene Tunney, actor Gary Cooper, philosopher Jean-Paul Sartre, matador Louis Miguel Dominguin, novelist Tennessee Williams, actor Spencer Tracy, heavyweight champion Rocky Marciano, and actress Marlene Dietrich.

But the legendary Constante was not the only talent who worked behind this bar. His cousin Antonio Meilan made his claim to fame when he finessed the recipe for the sugarless Daiquirí that he served to Ernest Hemingway, calling it Papa Doble.

PAPA DOBLE
60 ml Cuban rum
20 ml fresh grapefruit juice
15 ml fresh lime juice
10 ml maraschino liqueur
10 ml simple syrup
Shake ingredients over ice.
Strain into a chilled cocktail glass.

Head barman Salvador Trullols Mateu compiled and published, in 1927, the first edition of *The International Drink Book*. During the 1940s another barman, José Maria Vázquez, invented another enduring classic, the Daiquirí Mulata. And the tradition of service and cordial hospitality continues with current head barman Alejandro Bolivar.

DAIQUIRÍ MULATA

60 ml Cuban rum
15 ml white crème de cacao
15 ml dark crème de cacao
15 ml fresh lime juice
5 ml simple syrup
Frappé in a blender. Pour into
a chilled cocktail glass. Serve with
a small straw.

Hotel Florida

From the moment he arrived in Havana, in 1910, until his death in 1940, Spanish bartender Emilio "Maragato" González elevated the standards by which Cuban cocktails were made. Shaker at the ready, elegantly dressed in his white jacket, Maragato captured the hearts of every and anyone to arrived to pay homage to his mastery. He was famed for his Daiquirís which he served around 1913 at the Hotel Florida (and later at the Hotel Plaza) which according to Jaime Ariansen Cespedes were probably made with lime or key lime juice.[104]

One witness to Maragato's prowess at the Hotel Florida remarked: "…it was a small bar, and there was Maragato already the most famous barman in Havana: a Spaniard, medium height, stoutish, red-faced. grizzly-haired. He must have

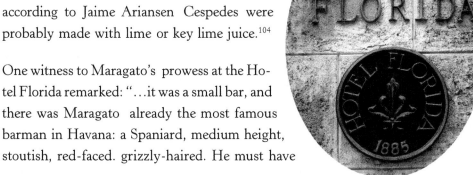

104 'La Historia Del Daiquirí: El Ciclón Del Caribe' (2012) <http://www. historiacocina. com/historia/articulos/Daiquirí.htm> accessed 2 February 2012.

been around forty, and was quite grave—not as jolly as Manteca— very elegant always with a white mess-jacket, always white."

Immediately after his death, his close connection to the Daiquirí became a point of controversy which we will discuss in a later chapter.

Sloppy Joe's

No less than 37 stools and all are occupied! Such was the impressive spectacle that lay before Sloppy Joe's two master cantineros. This perennially crowded bar on Animas Street between Prado and Zulueta Streets was a requisite destination from the 1930s to the 1950s for any visitor to Havana.

José Abeal y Otero arrived in Havana from Spain, in 1904, and took a bartending job at the corner of Galiano and Zanja Streets. Three years later, he packed his bags and set sail for New Orleans where he honed his bartending skills. Then he stopped in Miami where he continued to practice his craft.

Returning to Havana in 1918, José presided over the bar at the Greasy Spoon Café. Six months later he went into business with Valentin Garcia, opening a *bodega* [grocery store] at the same corner now occupied by Sloppy Joe's. Several of his old American friends visited him. Seeing the poor condition of the place, one of them remarked: "Why Joe, this place is certainly sloppy. Look at the filthy water running from under the counter."[105] Thus a name and a legend were born.

105   Sloppy Joe's Cocktail Manual (1st edn, Sloppy Joe's 1936) 5

Nestled between the fashionable Hotel Plaza and Sevilla-Biltmore Hotel, José and Valentin initially sold liquor and sundry groceries. Business developed rapidly and in a very short time, they built the elongated bar and the floor-to-ceiling liquor cabinets that occupied three walls.

Another legend grew around Sloppy Joe's reputation.

One day, an American journalist who lost a wad of money during a drinking session was quite moved and grateful to find his wallet and its entire contents at the bar the next day.

Thanks to this news item, American servicemen based in San Antonio de los Banos made Sloppy Joe's one of their regular hangouts [*see above*]. As soon as they arrived, the GIs put their money on the bar and started ordering drinks. As drinks were served, the cantineros drew payment from the stack until the funds ran out or the drinkers staggered out.

"Daiquirís and Piña Con Ron were the favourite orders," recalled Fabio Delgado, one of Sloppy Joe's most talented cantineros. "We made them in gigantic shakers and sometimes we made as many as a hundred at a time. The customers loved that and would order a round for the whole house!" This was an idiosyncrasy of the exuberant American millionaire Amelia Rusakoe, who made Sloppy Joe's her headquarters.

Delgado crafted such enduring concoctions as the Cuba Bella, Cubanacán, Negroni Especial, and Sol y Sombra during his 25 years of service.

CUBA BELLA

15 ml spearmint syrup
15 ml grenadine syrup
15 ml fresh lime juice
45 ml 3-year old rum
15 ml 7-year old rum

Pour spearmint syrup in the base of a hurricane glass, fill with cube ice. Shake the lime juice, grenadine, and 3-year old rum, strain, and layer over the spearmint syrup. Top with 7-year rum. Garnish with an orange slice, mint sprig, and a cherry.

For four decades, rich, famous and anonymous clients gathered for Sloppy Joe's giant cocktails—made with its own proprietary-label rum—and listened to the strains of "Vereda Tropical" and other languorous boleros played by the house trovadores. Actors Clark Gable, John Wayne, and Spencer Tracy were a few of the Hollywood A-listers who regularly bellied up to this mahogany bar.

The fame of Sloppy Joe's inspired the opening , in 1933, of Sloppy Joe's in Key West, Florida, by Joe Russell. Originally called the Silver Slipper, Ernest Hemingway strongly urged Russell to change the name to Sloppy Joe's.

The Sloppy Joe's sandwich [see above] which has a reputation of its own is a simple variation on Ropa Vieja served on a bun. In kind, Joe Russell created an Americanised version that became a staple in the American diet. Closing in 1965, this iconic reopened in 2013 as a popular locals hangout.

La Bodeguita del Medio

It is not the oldest altar to classic Havana cocktails. But La Bodeguita del Medio [*see below*] is certainly one of the most famous in the annals of Cuban rum history.

Its story begins in 1942 when the son of modest farmers named Angel Martinez purchased an old, rustic *bodega* named La Complaciente on Calle Empedrado in Old Havana. Patiently, Angel Martinez renovated the shop himself and renamed it Casa Martinez. He catered to his neighbours' needs, selling rum, soda, rice, and beans. That was fine, until 1946, when he met his new neighbour, publisher Felito Ayon. Because he produced the influential magazine *Arte y Literatura*, Havana's avant garde were both his business and his social circle. As he recalled: "I met Angel Martinez as soon as I set up in Calle Empedrado. Since I didn't have a phone yet, I called my clients from Casa Martinez. At that time it was a simple grocery store, but Angel also served refreshments. Little by little, I began taking my visitors there for a drink."

Two years later, Ayon and Martinez solidified a close friendship. the publisher was invited to partake in a traditional criollo lunch cooked by Martinez's wife Armenia. A plate of *masas de cerdo* [fried pork chunks with garlic] and *moros y cristianos* [rice with black beans] cost a mere peso. Angel accepted no more than that.

But how did this establishment get its name?

Ayon phoned a friend one day to ask her to lunch: "Meet me in the *bodeguita* [little cellar] in the *medio* [middle] of the block." Soon he and all his friends referred to Martinez's place by this now-familiar phrase of endearment. The unassuming owner gave in to their insistence and renamed his place La Bodeguita del Medio.

Many of Havana's best drinking establishments and luxury hotels offered Mojitos in those days: La Concha, Floridita, El Central. Yet Martinez's particular recipe for Mojitos captured the hearts and palates of novelist Ernest Hemingway [*see above*], performer Nat King Cole, actor Errol Flynn, writer Gabriel Garcia Marquez, and actress Brigitte Bardot, maintaining its international adoration to this day.

The Rooftop Bar at the Hotel Sevilla

Prohibition closed the curtain on America's Golden Age of Cocktails, but not before a young, well-trained generation of bartenders honed their skills behind the mahogany at landmark spots such as the Hoffman House and Hotel Knickerbocker. Many of America's bar legends from that memorable era were born in Germany such as Harry Johnson and Willy Schmidt, or were first-generation German-Americans such as Henry C Ramos and Eddie Woelke. It is this young barman who draws our attention.

Born in Philadelphia in 1877, Eddie worked in of the world's finest watering holes. From the Germantown Cricket Club in his hometown he made his way to the Plaza Athenée in Paris, where he met his wife Marcelle. Returning to the USA, he took a post in New York's Hotel Knickerbocker, in 1906, with a young British transplant named Harry Craddock (later of Savoy Hotel fame) and restaurant/bar manager James B. Regan.

When hotel's owner John Jacob Astor IV died in the tragic maiden voyage of the *Titanic*, on 15 April 1912, the hotel was handed over to his son Vincent. Possibly the change of ownership did not suit

Woelke, who took a post down the street, in 1913, at the New York Biltmore Hotel which opened on New Year's Day.

Just as Prohibition loomed on the horizon, luck sided with Eddie.

The Biltmore's owners John McEntee Bowman and Charles Francis Flynn had purchased the Sevilla Hotel on Calle Trocadero in Havana, in 1919, renaming it the Sevilla-Biltmore Hotel [*see opposite and above*]. Eddie was transferred there as part of the opening team.

Woelke shared the mahogany at this new venue with Fred Kaufman. He may never have written a cocktail book but Basil Woon immortalised Kaufman with the following description: "...originally of Liverpool, but a traveler of the Tropics so long that he talks English with a Spanish accent. Kaufman is never happy unless he is on an island. He was born on one, and has since worked in Funchal,

Madeira, and the Canary Islands. Kaufman is the inventor of several cocktails in which pineapple juice is the chief ingredient…"

His most enduring creation was crafted for silent screen star Mary Pickford.[106] The drink embodies simplicity and a comprehensive understanding go two Cuban ingredients: rum and pineapple.

MARY PICKFORD (1928 VERSION)
2/3 pineapple juice
1/3 rum
1 dash grenadine
Shake ingredients over ice and strain into a cocktail glass.

More often than not, another drink from the era—the Dorothy Gish Cocktail, named after another silent film star—is also attributed to Woelke, not Kaufman. But the profile alludes to Kaufman's authorship.

DOROTHY GISH NO. 2 (1948 VERSION)
½ oz white rum
½ oz apricot brandy
2 spoonfuls orange juice
Shake ingredients over ice and strain into a cocktail glass.[107]

These are not, by all means, the only bars that contributed to putting Havana on the drinks map as a mecca to cocktails. We'll mention a few more landmarks in a later chapter that's dedicated to the origins of a few Cuban classics.

106　　　Woon 40

107　　　H.A. Sanchez, El Arte Del Cantinero O Los Vinos Y Los Licores. (1st edn, P Fernandez y Cia 1948) 382

Even after the American bartenders and bar owners packed up and returned home to the mainland, the legacy of Cuban bars continued well into the 1940s and 1950s as evidenced by a list of famous Havana establishments which was published in 1949:[108]

- Amando, Hotel Inglaterra

- La Arboleda, Hotel Nacional, Vedado

- Acquarium, Industria no. 8, Old Havana

- Ariete, Consulado and San Miguel

- Bahía, Ave. del Puerto and Callejón de Justiz

- Bacardí, Edificio Bacardí, Ave de las Misiones between Empedrado and San Juan de Dios, Old Havana [*see above*]

- La Bodeguita del Medio, Empedrado no. 207, Old Havana

- Bodegón de Toyo, 10 de Octubre no. 370, Víbora Park

- Carmelo, Calzada and D, Vedado

- Colony, 21 and D, Vedado

- Chez Merito, Calzada and G, Vedado

- Daytona Club, Amistad no. 306

- Las Delicias de Medina, L and 21, Vedado

- Doce y Veintitrés, 23 and 12, Vedado

---

108 'Mesa Para Cuántos, Señor?' [1949] *Revista Desfile*. 4-5

- El Chalet, 12 and 23, Vedado

- El Encanto, Galiano and San Miguel

- Europa, Aguiar y Obispo, Old Havana

- Floridita, Obispo and Monserrate, Old Havana

- Golden Garden Club, 21 and N, Vedado

- Havana Club, Plaza de la Catedral, Old Havana [*see opposite*]

- Indian Bar, Hotel Sevilla-Biltmore

- Isla, Galiano and San Rafael

- Jardín, C and Línea, Vedado

- Kasalta, Ave. de las Américas

- La Concha, Playa de Marianao

- Longchamps, Hotel Sevilla-Biltmore

- Lucero, Calle Cuba, Old Havana

- Mar y Tierra, Padre Varela and Lagunas

- Mario's Club, San Miguel and Industria

- Morocco Night Club, Neptuno and San Miguel

- Montmartre Night Club, 23 and P, Vedado

- Palermo Club, San Miguel and Amistad

- Pan American Bar, Bernaza and O'Reilly, Old Havana

- La Panera, Tte. Rey and San Ignacio

- Patio, Paseo de Martí and Genio

- Petit Miramar, Miramar, Playa

- Plaza, Zulueta and Neptuno

- Prado 86, Paseo de Martí

- Puerto de Sagua, Egido and Acosta, Old Havana

- Reguladora, Amistad between Barcelona and Dragones

- Salón H, Manzana de Gómez

- Sea Club, Águila and Reina

- Siglo XX, Neptuno and Padre Varela

- Sloppy Joe's, Ánimas and Zulueta

- Templete, Ave. del Puerto and Narciso López

- Toledo, Águila and Barcelona

- Tony's Club, Hotel Regina, Industria no. 109

- Torreón, Ave. Washington and Malecón

- Tres Ases, Prado between Neptuno and Virtudes

- Tres Cepas, Aguacate and San Juan de Dios

- Tropicana Night Club, Ave 72, N° 4504, Marianao

- 23 y 12, 23 and 12, Vedado

- Victoria, 6 and Línea, Vedado

- Vista Alegre, Belascoaín and San Lázaro

- Wall Street, Aguiar and Obrapía, Old Havana

- Zaragozana, Monserrate between Obispo and Obrapía, Old Havana

Another Sort of American Invasion

Wait. Did we just say "after the American bartenders and bar owners packed up and went home? Why yes. We did. Cuba gained formal independence, on 20 May 1902, from both its Spanish rulers and its temporary American overseers. The island transformed itself almost overnight from a forgotten colony to a nation; from a staging post for gold seekers to the centre of the world's sugar production; from idle distiller to style maker that transformed the way people perceived rum on a global scale.

Cuba was not always a weathered time capsule of a bygone era. Once it was among the wealthiest nations in the world. During the late 1890s, it was already known as the "pearl of the Antilles", "the land of golden opportunity". Havana was sometimes referred to as the "Paris of the Caribbean".

Cuba's wealth was simple to explain. One-third of the world's sugar came from Cuba. During the late 1800s, the island had an estimated 13,000,000 acres of untouched mahogany forests. Annual exports included 250,000,000 cigars to the United States alone. Agriculture boomed beyond sugar and tobacco with burgeoning exports of bananas, grain, citrus fruits, coffee, cocoa, coconuts, and india rubber, too.[109]

Think of the size of the world and then consider the size of Cuba: the island is 760 miles long and 55 miles wide, making it slightly smaller than the state of Pennsylvania. Add up the influx of foreign money from exports and you catch a glimpse of Cuba's riches. Havana was the Dubai of its time, attracting the world's wealthiest to do business and to relax amid tropical splendour. Mansions sprang up along the coast, in the cities, and along the island wherever plantation owners decided to erect their dream homes.

Restaurants, hotels, clubs, bars, museums, theatres, and endless shopping streets followed. Tourists, those who could afford a visit, streamed into Havana and Trinidad and Santiago de Cuba. With them came foreign journalists and travel writers, enticing still more tourism.

Just before independence was won, American business interests on the island proliferated. Cuba's rich resources of iron ore, nickel, cobalt, feldspar, limestone, lime, asphalt, petroleum, tobacco, and sugar tantalised powerful magnates such as JP Morgan and Charles Rand of the Spanish-American Iron Company.[110] The United States government established a naval base on Guantánamo Bay, in 1898, and was granted a perpetual lease on the property five years later.

American soldiers, journalists, workers, tourists flocked to Cuba. They needed places where they could sleep, places where they could eat, places where they could drink. Hotels cropped up with modern

---

109   The Valentine Democrat, 'Cuban War Review. Two Years Of Fighting With Little Result''' (1897) 6

110   Cuba was considered in 2011 to be the world's seventh largest producer of cobalt and eighth largest producer of nickel, as reported in the *US Geological Survey's Minerals Yearbook—Area Reports: International Review: 2011, Latin America and Canada.*

conveniences such as electricity, elevators, hot-and-cold-running water, furnished in the "American style".[111]

A fleet of bars opened, in 1899, including the Washington Saloon, Yankee Bar, Texas Bar, New York Bar, and New England Bar. The Manhattan Bar followed a year later.[112]

Americans took a strong interest in Cuban rum, especially the servicemen who were stationed on the island. On leave, they packed into taverns and bars in Santiago de Cuba and Havana to get their fill of Daiquirís, Saocos, Cancháncharras, and Piña Coladas. Not just the privates and corporals took a fancy to rum. Enamoured with the Daiquirí after he was introduced to it by Jennings S Cox Jr. during the Spanish-Cuban War, Admiral Lucius W Johnson brought the recipe home to the Army & Navy Club in Washington DC, in 1909, and imported a generous stock of Cuban rum for his personal consumption.

University of North Carolina Professor of History Louis A Pérez Jr gave the most accurate description of the American bartender invasion that struck Havana at the dawn of Prohibition: "unemployed bartenders and saloon keepers found jobs in Havana as bars and cabarets that closed in the united States were reopened in Cuba. William Caldwell's Neptuno Bar...Harry McCabe's Golden Dollar Bar...Tom Morris from Cleveland owned the American Busy Bee Bar...Pat Cody also reopened his New York saloon, Jigg's uptown Bar...John Moller from Brooklyn opened Ballyhoo Bar...George Harris operated George's Winter Palace...Harry McGabe opened the Rialto Café, along on the Prado. ...The Seminole Café offered "nothing but genuine American and Scotch whiskey. Best draught

111   Louis A Pérez, On Becoming Cuban (1st edn, University of North Carolina Press 1999) 125

112   Perez 125

beer in town."[113] The U.S. Bar gave patrons free souvenir photos of their visit. [*see right*]

The Irish-American saloon tradition arrived on Cuban shores when Ed Donovan, who hailed from Newark, New Jersey, moved to Havana at the inception of Prohibition. He opened Café Donovan off the Parque Central, bringing his chairs, tables, mirrors, hanging sign, and the bar itself to the island lock stock and barrel.[114] A welcome home away from home for American ex-pats and tourists, the non-hotel style of bartending entered into the Cuban fabric. As reporter put it: "In the meantime, Café Donovan, as the American Bar is other wise known, is headquarters for many of the Americans living in Cuba, especially the ones domiciled there. ... Real American cooking is to be had and all the mixed drinks that used to be popular in the States can be obtained in their pristine

---

113 Perez 168

114 Conflicting sources from the period placed the bar at the Telegrafo Hotel or across the square at the Plaza Hotel.

perfection, for there is no lack of materials from which to compound them, nor of cunning hands to properly agitate them."[115]

The same reporter critically compared the American-owned bars to the Cuban-owned "saloons" by noting that: "It is these saloons along San Isidro street about which I particularly want to write. They have no swinging doors, like real saloons, or modern bootlegging joints in the states—in fact, they have no doors at all, the width of the bar and table space being open to the street, often on two sides. ...But that's not the feature of these saloons, either. It is the barmaids—comely young girls of all ages who serve the tired and thirsty traveler with the best the bar affords the minute he is seated at one of the tables."[116]

Hints of New Orleans bar culture arrived around the same time. Greek emigrants Constantino (aka: "Billy") and Peter Economides opened the Café Sazerac around the corner from the Hotel Inglaterra Bar & Patio.[117] Peter had been head barman at the New Orleans Café on 42nd street near Times Square in New York, where he had earned a reputation for making his own version of a Ramos Gin Fizz.[118]

The flood of American bartenders emigrating to Cuba was noted in the stateside newspapers, precisely one month after Prohibition was in full swing: "...former saloon keepers and bartenders of Chicago are going down to Havana at a rate of 12 a day, according to Jacob Poppet, Internal Revenue deputy collector. 'While many of these men are going down on pleasure trips,' he said, 'there is no doubt that some of them are going there to open saloons and prepare for

---

115   C.L. Murray, 'Havana Described As An Americanized Old World Place; Who Is Donovan?' Galveston Daily News (1922)

116   ibid.

117   Woon 43

118   Perez 168-173

the great American rush. They want to be on hand when the private stocks in the cellars are gone.'"[119]

It wasn't just the bartenders that were hightailing it to Havana. A few distilleries and breweries relocated to the island as well. W A Kennerly moved his distillery from Roanoke, Virginia to Cuba. "The Havana Distilling Company— which represents considerable American capital," reported the USA chargé d'affaires Edward Reed, "opened a large plant at El Cano to manufacture rye whiskey, Scotch, and other liquors."[120] The Cuba Cervercera Company purchased, in 1920, the entire factory of the US Brewing Company of Chicago, increasing its production capacity to five million litres of beer daily.[121]

But as with all people who come to Cuba, these barmen were influenced at least as much as they themselves influenced local cocktail culture. They too came away with a part of Cuba in their souls, especially when a new generation of Cuban bartenders arose. This change of personnel was the final element to effecting the perfect balance—the perfect cocktail for an enduring, internationally relevant cocktail tradition which we like to call the Golden Age of Cuban Cocktails.

---

119   Elgin Echo, 'Saloon Men Go To Cuba: Twelve A Day Sail For Havana, Says United States Internal Revenue Deputy At Chicago' (1920)

120   Perez 169

121   ibid.

The Club de Cantineros de Cuba Is Born

An American invasion was the reason why Cuban *cantineros* united. The very second Prohibition in the USA closed the doors on bars from coast to coast, a flood of American bartenders headed to Cuba to ply their trade.

Aside from the Sevilla-Biltmore Hotel's acquisition and upgrade in both 1919 and 1924 by John M Bowman, other American hoteliers came to Havana during the 1920s to open establishments designed to accommodate the influx of American tourists. Naturally, American bartenders followed the bar owners to go where the work was more than available, it was plentiful.[122]

Walter Fletcher modelled his Hotel Plaza after New York's opulent Plaza Hotel. W T Burbridge opened the Miramar. Dwight Hughes launched the Albany Hotel. John A Richardson welcomed guests at the Hotel Lincoln.[123] Others followed: the Hotel Vanderbilt, Hotel Packard, Hotel Cecil, St Louis Hotel, Hotel Biscuit, Hotel Bristol, Savoy Hotel, Hotel Saratoga, Hotel Pacific, Hotel Palace, Boston Hotel, Miami Hotel, Hotel Parkview, Hotel Ambassador, Hotel Washington, Hotel Seminole, Clifton House, and the New Ritz Hotel.[124]

No to be out gunned by American entrepreneurial enthusiasm, Cuban and Spanish businessmen who catered to American tastes opened American-style hotels, cabarets, and eateries such as Ramón Rodríguez's Armenonville Cabaret; Segundo González's Hotel Harding; Vicente Castro's Hotel Chicago; José Valiela's Hotel

---

122   Kokomo Tribune, 'Bartenders Leaving' (1920); Carbondale Daily Free Press, 'Yank Bartenders Leaving' (1920).

123   Perez 168-173

124   ibid.

Pennsylvania; Francisco García's Park House Hotel; Antonio Villanueva's Hotel Manhattan; José Morgado's Hotel New York; plus Teodoro Miranda's Hotel Ohio, Telégrafo Hotel, Gran Hotel América, and Hotel Almendares.[125]

As we mentioned earlier, Spanish barman José Abeal y Otero opened Sloppy Joe's, in 1920, fresh from honing his skills in New Orleans.

Francisco and Gustavo del Barrio opened the New York Bar. Benito "Benny" Rego managed the Winter Garden Bar.[126]

But it was the plight of one Spanish bartender who emigrated to Cuba in search of work struck a very sour note with Spanish ex-pats such as Maragato. Madrid-trained barman Elisayo Castro couldn't find work in Cuba's hundreds of new cafés, bars, and hotels because he couldn't speak English, let alone mix drinks in the American style. Nearly every available job was taken by American barmen—many of them members of the "International Bartenders' Union of the United States".[127] Desperate for work, Castro stowed away on a passenger ship headed to New York City. He was discovered and sent to Ellis Island along with four other stowaways.

What every one of these new Havana establishments promised its growing customer base was true American service, real American cuisine, real American drinks, and staff that spoke American English.

Cuban barmen heard the call for action.

---

125 Perez 168-173

126 ibid.

127 The Washington Post, 'Wants To Learn Mixology' (1920). Please note, that there are no records of the existence of an International Bartenders' Union of the United States documented anywhere.

There was a labour organisation that included bartenders amongst its membership, since 1912, named the Unión de Empleados de Café. But the body did not effectively defend bartenders in the wake of this American industrial invasion. Divisions emerged. Barman Perales José Mora suggested, in late 1923, the establishment of an independent Sección de Cantina. Initially, his concept fell on deaf ears. But a few months later, the new section was headed by a professional barman who had no political ties named Manuel Blanco Cuétara.[128]

According to some versions of the story, political intrigue plagued the new organisation and its leader until Mora united forces with José Cuervo Fernandez and Cristobal Alonso Fernandez. The trio wrote and published a manifesto that was circulated amongst the city's bar staff.

Bartenders met, on 9 May 1924, in the billiard room at Hotel Ambos Mundos to compile a series of regulations written by Manuel Blanco Cuétara and drafted by attorney Manuel Zavala.[129]

After a couple of interim meetings, the final version of the organisation's charter was approved by the government on 27 June 1924, registering El Club de Cantineros de la Republica de Cuba [*see opposite*] in the Special Register of Associations with Hotel Ambos Mundos's José Cuervo Fernandez as president and Cristóbal Blanco Alvarez as secretary-general.[130]

Within its first six months, the club recruited 121 members.[131]

---

128   H.A. Sanchez, *Memoria: 25 Años De Labor Del Club De Cantineros De La Republica De Cuba* (1st edn, Compañia Editora de Libros y Folletos 1951). 5-7

129   ibid.

130   Libro 16, Folio 288, No. 5415 Cf: Archivo Nacional de Cuba, Fondo Registro de Asociaciones, Leg. 305, No. 54, Exp. 8851; Hector Zumbado, *A Barman's Sixth Sense* (1st edn, Cubaexport 1980) 33.

131   Sanchez 5-7

The membership had funding for a meeting house at Malécon No.15 and attempted in those early days to publish a magazine. But political infighting and outside agitation from other hospitality unions kept the fledgling group from making any serious advances. It also didn't help that when Presidente Gerardo Machado took office, in 1925, he was hostile to any type of labour organisation.[132]

The group moved its headquarters to Paseo del Prado No. 105 (aka: Avenida de Martí) and established a mandatory 1 AM closing time.

To improve its public image, all games were banned except for pool and dominoes.[133]

Subsidised by local distilleries, brasseries, and liquor merchants, the club served several roles: as a trade union that defended the cantineros' professional interests; as a guild that provided English courses for apprentices; as a gathering place that nurtured the health and

---

132 Sanchez 5-7

133 ibid.

well-being of its members with a library, a jai-alai court, billiard room, and bathing facilities.[134]

Visible signs of a welling pride in the profession of cocktail emerged. Cocktail books were published.

El Arte de Hacer un Cocktail y Algo Mas presented hundreds of drink recipes, classified by category was published, in 1927, by Compañia Cervecera Internacional in Havana. As mentioned earlier, the first edition of Salvador Trullols Mateu's *The International Cocktail Book* [*see left*] was also published that same year. This Catalan emigrant had become head bartender at El Floridita. And as one Spanish barman reminisced years later: "At 15, I was given a cocktail book, published in Havana back in 1927, written by Salvador Trullols Mateu (...) I was intrigued so that after three months I knew it all by heart. His whole theory of the world. ..."[135]

With the elections of Manuel Alvarez Alvarez as association president and Cándido López Guitián as secretary general, in 1928, a new article was added to the club's charter on 14 June: "ARTICLE 1—. Was constituted in the Republic of Cuba and indefinite Club

134   Anistatia Miller and Jared Brown, Interview with Elio Moya, 'Interview With Former President Of The Club Del Cantineros De Cuba' (2008)

135   "'Enrique Bastante, Campeon Del Mundo' [1994] *Revista EPICUR* 128

de Cantineros de la Republic de Cuba composed of a few elements of morality and decency in fighting their existence in canteens, cafés, eateries, bars, restaurants, and hotels, with the moral and material effort of its personal work. Its mission is: Laboring for the intellectual, economic, and moral benefit of all its partners…"[136]

Naturally, older trade groups who counted bartenders amongst their memberships harboured animosity toward this new upstart organisation. Centro Internacional de Cocineros, Sociedad Cubana de Dependientes de Restaurantes Hoteles y Fondas de la Ciudad de La Habana, and Unión de Dependientes de Café were the most vocal.[137] They even publicly accused the club of being a front for illegal gambling in the magazine *Federacion* as well as in a speech delivered at an assembly of hospitality organisations.[138] In the end, the club did not win complete independence from the federated hospitality unions. But it did win the right to exist as its own entity.[139]

Havana's workforce had to give the public what they wanted: standardised recipes that appealed to the American palate; service that equalled or surpassed what could be found in the USA or Europe; workers who could speak English; and an unrivalled sense of personal style.[140] The club published its first manual of standardised recipes in that inaugural year, written by León Pujol and Oscar Muñiz.[141]

---

136   Archivo Nacional de Cuba, Fondo registro de Asociaciones, Leg.305, No. 54, Exp. 8851, folio 85

137   Sanchez 40

138   Sanchez 44-45

139   ibid

140   Anistatia Miller and Jared Brown, Interview with Elio Moya, 'Interview With Former President Of The Club Del Cantineros De Cuba' (2008)

141   L. Pujol and O Muñiz, *Manual Del Cantinero* (1st edn, Guillermo Librero 1924) 1-56

Nine years before the United Kingdom Bartenders Guild (frequently cited as the world's first bartender's association) was established by a group of London bartenders, the club set about to train a new generation of Cuban-born professions to live up to journalist Hector Zumbado's eloquent description: "They have the elegance of a symphony conductor, the precision and calm of a surgeon ready to operate. They are the chemists of today, the botanists of the eighteenth century, the alchemists of the Middle Ages, capable of willing the creation of cool, shining gold. They are experts in the topics of sport and international politics, but they never give in to passionate discourse. ...They need the memory of elephants for they must remember how to make, without looking them up, between 100 and 200 cocktails. ...Such a man exists. He is the Barman, imaginative and creative, a craftsman in ice, a poet of potions, imbued with a true love for his work. He has his own personality and style. He puts something of himself, of his innermost self into every drink he prepares: part of him is in it, giving it life. ...His five senses are superbly tuned. And he has a sixth sense: the sense of cocktail-making."[142]

A club publication that was distributed during the 1930s pointed out that: "A source of pride to us are the theoretical-practical lectures and the cocktail-making classes...These classes have resulted in the Cuban barman's being considered the best-trained of all the barmen in the world today."[143] Agreeing with this, Albert Stevens Crockett said in his 1935 volume *Old Waldorf-Astoria Bar Book*: "Cuba is the most advanced country in cocktail-making today; American, English, and French barmen have a lot to learn here."[144]

Prohibition in the USA ended with the ratification of the 21st Amendment to the USA Constitution, on 5 December 1933, which repealed the 18th Amendment. Yet, the mass migration of

---

142   Zumbado 40

143   Zumbado 33

144   ibid.

American bartenders to Havana did not immediately reverse. There was tourist money to be had in Cuba. Why go back to the United States? Cuban bartenders faced a major problem.

The Fight for the Profession

American tourism waned slightly because drink could once again be sipped on home shores. But PanAm Airlines and numerous cruise ships continued to press for travel to Cuba despite the change in circumstance. They didn't want to lose their share of an extremely profitable cash pie. The association focussed its attention on training local barmen to serve this continuing influx of American and European tourists.

The club initiated, the previous year in 1932, an educational series titled *Conferencias Teórico-Prácticas sobre el Arte del Cantinero*. Bartenders were trained in practical and theoretical bartending skills. They were offered English classes, giving them an edge in the job market against the American barmen who still lingered in Cuba.

Soon the club was also credited for its labours as a workers' defence organisation, speaking on behalf of as well as organising strikes and boycotts against the cabaret Eden Concert, in June 1934, as well as the Hotel Inglaterra's bars Regina and Spanish Tavern.[145]

Friction was inevitable. American bartenders who were threatened with deportation by the government joined other outraged Cuban barmen in strike actions. Fulgencio Batista y Zaldívar rose to power during the 1933 Revolt of the Sergeants that had overthrown

---

145 Sanchez 137-144

Presidente Gerardo Machado. He effectively controlled the five-member presidency during this delicate period.

In an effort to support labour unions, the government passed the "Law of 50%" which mandated that one half of the personnel in any Cuban business—or the membership of a labour union, a guild, and even the club—had to be Cuban nationals. At this stage, one observer commented: "... It became impossible for [North] American employment. The American firms were very angry when they learned that the British government had inserted a clause in the Treaty of Commerce with Cuba, authorising British firms to 'employ a rational number of nationals'." The American government had made no provisions to protect their citizens in a similar fashion.[146]

American barmen who had not bothered to join the club were asked to leave the island. Some begrudgingly departed. Others who arrived just before repeal found no work and were consequently glad to return home. The Cuban hospitality market was saturated. The club had fulfilled the demand for bartenders with local talent.

The club's most important win, in 1936, put an end to the American bartender invasion and proved to be the ultimate retribution for the plight of Elisayo Castro. The club obtained—and in many cases even paid for—Letters of Naturalisation for more than 180 of its foreign members, especially those who were Spanish-born.[147]

A fully-formalised version of the two-year-old educational series was launched, on 13 August 1934, and titled *Clases de Coctelería Práctica*. It was the precursor to the 90-day course that became the standard curriculum—*Escuela Técnica Profesional del Cantinero*.

---

146   R. Hart Phillips, *Cuba, Island Of Paradox* (McDowell, Obolensky 1959).

147   Sanchez 162-165

But it was the final establishment of the *Concurso de Cocteleria,* on 24 October 1935, that consecrated the association's credentials. The first competition took place on 24 November 1936 at association headquarters. The event was supported by the government, the major liquor companies, distilleries, Asociación de Industriales de Cuba, and Corporación Nacional de Turismo. There were 1,382 cocktail entries created by 164 *cantineros.* According to some sources, a newsreel film of the event was produced, which was distributed in both Cuba and the USA.[148] Each day was devoted to a specific category: vermouth, rum, cognac or champagne, gin, whisky, cups with and without alcohol, as well as so-called pluses.

This was also the year that Salvador Trullols Mateu's *The International Cocktail Book* was reissued in both Spanish and English. Plus Constante Ribalaigua Vert's book *Bar La Florida* also appeared for the first time.

Collective agreements between the club and the management at the Sevilla-Biltmore and Nacional Hotels, in 1938, ensured proper working conditions for *cantineros* at these last domains of ex-pat barmen Eddie Woelke and Fred Kaufman, who packed up and went home.

148 Sanchez 192

The Bible of Cuba's First Golden Age

The depth and breadth of the club's education programme is best evidenced in the 492-page revised edition of Hilario Alonso Sanchez's *El Arte del Cantinero* [*see below*]. This seminal volume covered the history of the bartending profession; provided detailed descriptions and histories of wines, beers, and spirits used

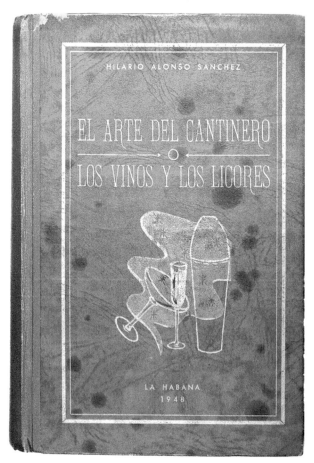

behind the bar; and recorded the origins of numerous classic cocktails.

Taking a page from Harry Johnson's 1888 *Bartenders' Manual*, the book lists the suggested inventory of spirits, wines, beers, and mixers that every bartender should stock. A detailed list of glassware and bar equipment is followed by recipes for making common bar syrups and a variety of canapés is accompanied by the "moral code" by which a *cantinero* must work. Naturally, the last 150 pages documented standardised recipes that were popular throughout Cuba and indeed the world.

After Nationalisation and onto the Future

Elio Moya Aguiar, [*see below*] head bartender at Eden Roc during the tumultuous 1950s, was the last president of Club de Cantineros, which by that time had 1,400 members.[149] Even after nationalisation, Moya represented the *cantineros* at governmental meetings.[150] It appears that, in 1959, the association's headquarters at Prado 111, (formerly No. 27) was nationalised.[151] A year later, the Escuela de Hoteleria was founded on the premises   o f the Gastronomic Union, the organisation that assumed a number of hospitality trade unions. It was moved again, in 1962, to the Hotel Sevilla. The training centre for all branches of hotel work also houses the *cantineros'* bartending school.[152]

Hector Zumbado provided the best description of the school, saying that: "If on a class day one goes up to the second floor and walks down the corridor to a room marked 'Aula de Bar', he will find a group of students neatly dressed in white, long-sleeved shirts with freshly starched collars, black trousers and ties, seated at their desks paying close attention to their instructor. ...Their teacher is Fabio

---

149   'Breves De La Historia' [2010] *El Coctel Azul*

150   Diario de la Marina, 'Cooperación De La Mujer Cubana A La Revolución' (1959) A6

151   "Breves de la Historia"

152   Zumbado 34

Delgado, grey-haired and bespectacled in his white smock, a veteran barman who started working in 1936 ("The youngest of the period," he recalls proudly), and who three years later—almost 40 years ago—received his Barman's Diploma."[153]

A revival and consequent new development in Cuban tourism during the 1990s led to an increased interest in Cuban cocktails on a global level. To answer the need for a high level of professionalism and customer service, the Club de Cantineros was officially reinstated, on February 1998, as a member of the International Bartenders Association (IBA) and a year later changed its name to the Asociación de Cantineros de Cuba. As it had in the past, the association continues to educate bar professionals through apprentice up to master level courses. The organisation also conducts regional and national competitions across the island to stimulate pride and communication amongst its membership. A national competition that is held annually to honour Fabio Delgado—who died on 7 February 2003—[see above] sends its first and second place winners to participate in the IBA's World Championships and Pan-American Competition.

The association has also played an integral role since 1996 in the biennial Havana Club Cocktail Grand Prix, which brings together talent from close to 50 countries to compete in Havana and celebrate the artistry of the Cuban cocktail tradition.

153   Zumbado 34-35

This passion, this mastery of skills and ingredients, this formation of a new and wholly Cuban style of bartending became more than an isolated, ethnocentric pastiche and continues to exert its influence today. Cuban bartending in its first golden age stretched out and embraced the world not only with an international array of tourists, but with two persuasive American restaurateurs who gave birth to a whole new category of mixed drink whose inspiration and execution blossomed from its Cuban roots.

Tiki Arises

The cantineros' influence on the bartending profession spread far beyond this island nation. Not only did American bartenders return to the USA with dozens of Cuban recipes. Not only did American and European tourists request those same drinks upon their return from a Cuban holiday.

Born in Mexia, Texas, Ernest Raymond Beaumont Gantt got his first taste of travel in September 1914 when at the age of seven, he took a bus to Mandeville, Louisiana to live with his grandfather. Before a month had past, Gantt sailed the Gulf of Mexico and the Caribbean with his lively relative. As he reminisced in later years: "But it was the travel that had me hook, line, and sinker. I lusted for other islands far away. Islands I had only heard tales of from sailors and drunks when Grandpappy and I would reach a new port, or sit in one of those old, broken-down bars Grandpappy loved in Haiti or Havana. Grandpappy was determined I would get an education equal to one provided by any university in the world, but a much more practical one."[154]

---

154   A Bitner, *Scrounging The Islands With The Legendary Don The Beachcomber: Host To Diplomat, Beachcomber, Prince And Pirate* (iUniverse 2007)

By the time Gantt left home to seek his fortune, in 1926, he knew well Havana's bars and sampled more than a few of its drinks. When he finished scouring the South Pacific and landed in Hollywood, in December 1931, he had assimilated enough Cuban culture to incorporate it seamlessly, two years later, into his establishment—Don's Beachcomber Café. [*see above*]

The seeds of Tiki were sown.

Vic Bergeron's first encounter with Cuban cocktails in Havana didn't occur as early in life or as colourfully as Gantt's. He opened Hinky Dink's, on 17 November 1934, in Oakland, California, along with his wife Esther Lynn. As he admitted in later years: "Although I knew quite a bit about cooking and could make all the routine cocktails, I didn't know very much about concocting fancy drinks, especially those with a tropical flavour. And this was an area where

I felt real imagination could be employed—and lots of fun could be had—in mixing and serving drinks."[155]

After two long, hard years building up the business, Vic and Esther packed their bags and headed to New Orleans. Learning a few tropical drinks from Albert Martin, owner of the Bon Ton Bar on Magazine Street, they then headed south to Havana.

Bergeron [see below] walked into La Florida where he introduced himself to Constante (whom he called Constantino Rapalo) and asked him how to make some of the bar's famous drinks. "When I went back to Oakland, I started to mix several different drinks. I used the La Florida [Rum Daisy] Cocktail, the La Florida Daiquirí, and a Planter's Punch, along with some of the drinks Albert Martin had shown me," Bergeron recalled. "And we went to work and made up a lot of new ones. Drinks that would sell in America."[156]

When Hinky Dink's reopened as Trader Vic's, in 1937, classic Cuban cocktails and Americanised Cuban drinks were on the menu. Within a few years, Tiki was well on its way. Vic reached further than his friend/rival Gantt, opening stateside restaurants in Beverly Hills, Boston, Chicago, Dallas, Detroit, Houston, Kansas City, Los Angeles, and New York in addition to venues in Europe and Puerto Rico. Then Vic's love of Cuban flavours came full-circle when Conrad Hilton asked him

---

155 Trader Vic., Frankly Speaking: Trader Vic's Own Story (1st edn, Doubleday 1973) 42

156 Trader Vic 43-44

to open a Trader Vic's, in 1958, at the hotelier's newest venture, the Havana Hilton.[157] Now called the Habana Libre Hotel, Vic's establishment still stands, which was renamed Polinesio [*see above*].

Gantt's Don the Beachcomber restaurant also enjoyed overwhelming success, albeit only within the United States. Between 1934 and 1979, Beach spread the word about Tiki from coast to coast, opening Don the Beachcomber restaurants not only in Hollywood, but in Chicago, Dallas, Denver Houston, Las Vegas, Honolulu, Malibu, Seattle, Waikiki, Palm Springs, St. Paul, two in San Diego, and one in West Lafayette, Louisiana. Even more suburban outlets appeared in Aurora, Colorado, as well as California coastal communities, including Corona del Mar, Marina del Rey, Oxnard, Santa Barbara, Santa Clara, and the Disney California Adventure Park. Today, only a Huntington Beach establishment on the Pacific Coast Highway remains.

---

157   Trader Vic 76

Few people realise how many classic cocktails were invented in Cuba, beyond the Mojito, Daiquirí, and Cuba Libre. A quick flight from Miami to Cuba or a fishing trip on the Gulf of Mexico or the Caribbean brought a thirsty traveler to the "world's loveliest playground", the haven of El Presidentes, Mulatas, Cubanitos, Mary Pickfords, Havana Specials, and a precursor to Piña Coladas—Saocos.[158]

SAOCO

In a tall (10 oz) highball glass:
2 oz Havana Club Light Dry
4 oz coconut water
ice cubes or cracked ice.
Stir and serve with a straw' (This drink looks and tastes better if served in the coconut itself.[159]

It was a particularly welcome sight for parched patrons during Prohibition in the USA. The stories surrounding these drinks have been passed down from bartender to bartender, from sipper to sipper, transforming many times into nothing more than romantic hearsay.

So what are the truths and factions about some of Cuba's legendary classic drinks?

---

158 Louis A Pérez, *Cuba In The American Imagination* (1st edn, Univ of North Carolina Press 2008) 233

159 Zumbado 55

Chapter Five

CUBAN
CLASSICS

Before the 1959 Revolution, Havana was America's "local bar." Stateside publications fanned the flames of desire before, during, and after Prohibition closed the doors on the American bartending profession. *Travel Magazine*, in 1922, mentioned a rum-based cocktail consumed in Cuba since the nineteenth century, that was a global sensation by the 1950s, albeit in a different form: the Piña Colada was a simple blend of rum, fresh pineapple juice, and lime juice back in those early times.

Throughout the centuries, masterful *cantineros* served up a repertoire as legendary in its history as the icons of entertainment, literature, music, politics, and business who drank them. As sunset gives way to night, the hour of the *borrachera* [the intoxication of the soul] begins. The flattering pick-up lines for which Latin lovers are famed—locally called *piropos*—whispered from one debonair customer to a lovely other. With glass held high, a *brindis* [toast] applauds the *cantinero* for his creation. A *trovador* receives a *piropo* from a sultry listener whose heart echoes in murmurs the soft strum of his guitar.

Now, the stories of five classic drinks can be told.

Mojito: the Authentically Cuban Drink

A Cuban icon that is as popular (if not more so) as Brazil's national drink—the Caipirinha—the Mojito reputedly is one of the world's first mixed drinks. It proudly stands alongside the Mint Julep, which boasts an ancestry that spans from a sweetened medicinal preparation made by Arab physicians to an anti-malarial sipped by the French to a simple British stomach remedy.

In the 1753 edition of *The New Dispensatory*, a simple Stomach Julep called for six ounces of "simple mint water" (which the book later describes as a distillation of 1.5 pounds of dry mint leaves and water), two drams of saffron syrup, and two ounces of spirituous mint water made by distilling 1.5 pounds of dry mint leaves and 1 gallon of spirit.[160]

JULEPEUM STOMACHICUM[161]

180 ml "simple mint water"
(distilled mint water)
5 ml saffron syrup
60 ml spirituous mint water
Blend together and serve.

The reason that we mention this considerably earlier recipe for a Mint Julep is that it defends an assumption that British sailors and pirates may have known that mint is an excellent remedy for stomach disorders as far back as the Elizabethan times.

Why do we start our discussion with Mint Juleps? Because it offers a new insight into the origins of the Mojito's purported ancestor the Draque.

Fernando G Campoamor offered in his glossary to his book *El Hijo Alegre de la Caña de Azúcar* a hint as to the popularity, during the 1800s, of the "Draque", the alleged ancestor of the Mojito.[162]

The author points to Sir Francis Drake as the drink's inventor. In recent times, that designation has been rightfully handed Richard Drake who allegedly was at sea with the famed privateer and

---

160   W Lewis, *The New Dispensatory...Intended As A Correction, And Improvement Of...* (1st edn, J Nourse 1753) 379

161   Lewis 612

162   F.G. Campoamor, *El Hijo Alegre De La Caña De Azúcar* (1st edn, Editorial Científico-Técnica 1981) 134

crafted the drink to honour (or aid) his commander and close relation. But who was he?

Richard Drake of Esher, was the son of John and Anne (née: Grenville) Drake and first cousin to the famed navigator Sir Francis Drake. Yes. He worked with his cousin, taking charge of the Spanish Armada prisoners captured off the coast at Plymouth, in 1588, which included the Spanish vice-admiral, Don Pedro de Valdés, whom he kept at his manor of Esher in Surrey, pending arrangements for payment of a ransom. But he never went to sea with his cousin.

However, Francis Drake's nephew did go to sea.

Admiral Sir Richard Hawkins was the son of Admiral Sir John Hawkins and Sir Francis Drake's nephew. He was also a well-known "sea dog" [British privateer], who accompanied his uncle, in 1582, as Drake raided raid the Brazilian coast. Three years later, he captained one of the galliots[163] in Drake's fleet that scoured the Spanish Main from the Caribbean to the Gulf of Mexico.

According to some English accounts crews on all of his ships fell ill, in 1586, forcing him to postpone his plan to ransack Havana and secure a safe hideaway.[164]

Few British vessels left port without a few essential medical supplies such as the ingredients for mixing up a Stomach Julep made with local mint such as *hierbabuena* mixed some sort of spirit, either brandy or readily available *aguardiente de caña*, thanks to advice received from French corsairs and Maroons, who were slaves who escaped from their Caribbean sugar plantations.

---

163   A galliot is a single-masted Dutch cargo vessel.

164   Irene Aloha Wright, *Further English Voyages To Spanish America, 1583-1594* (1st edn, Printed for the Hakluyt Society 1951) 186-187

Campoamor noted that according to a dictionary of Spanish slang that was assembled in the late 1800s by Venezuelan linguist Lisandro Alvarado, the word *draque* is also associated with an aguardiente-based stomach remedy in Maracaibo, Venezuela—another of Drake's target ports. An "energetic herbal tisane" called drague also appeared in Mexico. The same drink offered relief from dehydration in Cartagena, Colombia—yet another Drake target.[165]

Even after Drake's death, in 1596, from dysentery after an unsuccessful attack on San Juan, Puerto Rico, his namesake potion lived on as the **draque, drague, draquecito, drak,** or **drac.**

DRAQUECITO
60 ml aguardiente
Sugar to taste
Combine ingredients and serve.

The drink's name and two main ingredients make an appearance in Ramón de Palma y Romay's 1838 novella *El Cólera en La Habana en 1833* in which a character remarks: *"Yo me tomo todos los días a las once un draquecito de aguardiente de caña con azúcar y me va perfectamente* [Every day at eleven o'clock I take my draquecito of aguardiente de caña with sugar and it suits me perfectly.]*[166]

A citrus component may have been added as drinks such as the seventeenth-century British Punch, Bajan Rum Punch from Barbados, Ti Punch in Martinique and other French-Caribbean colonies as well the nineteenth-century Canchánchara in Cuba were born.

However, author Fernando Ortiz quoted an article titled "La Boca del Moro" that was written by journalist Federico Villoch in the 28 October 1940 edition of *Diario de la Marina* that claims the lime

---

165 Campoamoar 134

166 ibid.

and mint were always part of the equation: "A good dose of aguardiente de caña, half a glass, with sugar, a little water, intoned with a few sprigs of hierbabuena and a wedge of lime. It was consumed as the draque until 1800 and its peak until it was displaced by Cuban rum and Holland gin." [167]

Historian and journalist Ciro Bianchi Ross believes that the Draquecito evolved into the "Mojito Batido", in 1910, when it first appeared in print. Historian Miguel Bonera Miranda narrates that the Mojito itself was born on the beach [*see above*]: "In the Bar of the Hotel-Balneario "La Concha", in Havana, a bar attendant called Rogelio created, in 1910, a combination of white Cuban rum, ice, pomelo or lemon juice, unrefined sugar, a few dashes of Angostura

---

167   F. Ortiz, *Contrapunteo Cubano Del Tabaco Y El Azucar* (1st edn, J Montero 1940) 31. Since the original Villoch article has not been located, it is difficult to determine if the journalist went on to say that: "When aguardiente is replaced with rum, the Draque is to be called a Mojito." This version of Villoch's statement has been circulated on the internet since 2006, when it appeared in a *Miami Herald* entry posted on 28 June 2006. Since then it has been picked up by numerous drinks blogs and even *Diffords Guide* includes it in its entry on the Mojito #1.

bitters and soda water which was baptised with the name of 'Mojito'. Some of them, later, tried to affirm that: '... it was born in the 1930s in the Sevilla Hotel, in Havana, by someone looking for a drink that was symbolised Cuba.'"[168]

LA CONCHA MOJITO
Cuban rum
Pomelo or lemon juice
unrefined sugar
Angostura bitters
Soda water
Build in a highball glass. Add a few cubes of ice. Serve with a straw.

Author Rafael Lam adds that: "In this club on Marianao beach, the demand for Mojitos was so great, that sometimes the bar would run out of lemons. Bartenders would them use pomelo juice instead. This variation was considered to be higher class and thus costlier.[169]

In effect, La Concha Mojito is a Rum Rickey, a rum version of a mixed-drink style that appeared in Washington DC, in 1883, and became a nationwide hit when the Gin Rickey was introduced in Chicago at the 1893 Columbian Exposition. Made with the juice and shell of half a lime and optional bitters (unlike its British ancestor, the Collins, which was made with lemon juice and optional bitters), the basic Rickey recipe is a prime example:

---

168   Miranda 522. It is possible that the people Miranda mentions were the same individuals who asserted that nearly every popular drink made in Havana was invented by Eddie Woelke while he was behind the bar at the Sevilla-Biltmore Hotel.

169   R Lam, *La Bodeguita Del Medio* (Editorial José Martí 1994).

WHISKEY RICKEY[170]
(use a medium size fizz glass.)
1 or 2 pieces of ice;
Squeeze the juice of 1 good-sized
lime or 2 small ones;
1 wine-glass of rye whiskey
Fill up the glass with club soda, selters,
or vichy; and serve with a spoon.

In the 1927 book *El Arte de Hacer un Cocktail y Algo Mas*, another drink named the Mojo Criollo makes an appearance:[171]

MOJO CRIOLLO (1927 VERSION)
Glass of rum
Drops of lemon juice
Spoonful of sugar
Serve in a medium glass with ice and a spoon.

Two similar recipes made their way overseas to the UK by the 1930s and were included in the 1937 Café Royal Cocktail Book: The Daiquirí Sour and the Daiquirí Fizz.[172]

DAIQUIRÍ SOUR (1937 VERSION)
Juice of ½ Lemon
1 teaspoon superfine sugar
1 glass Daiquirí Rum
Shake. Use champagne glass, add slice of orange and a cherry. Fill with soda water.

170 Harry Johnson, *The Bartenders' Manual, Revised Edition* (1st edn, Harry Johnson 1900) 171

171 *El Arte De Hacer Un Cocktail Y Algo Mas* (1st edn, Compañia Cervecera International SA 1927) 172

172 W. J Tarling, *Café Royal Cocktail Book* (1st edn, Pall Mall 1937) 219

DAIQUIRÍ FIZZ (1937 VERSION)

Juice of ½ Lemon or Lime
1 teaspoon superfine sugar
½ Daiquirí Rum
Shake and strain into tumbler, fill with soda water.

And in another section, a Ron Rickey and a Rum Rickey also make an appearance. Still no mint. Where's the mint!

In John B Escalante's 1915 *Manuel del Cantinero* a Mint Julep and a Ron Bacardí Julep are about as close as it gets to marrying rum and mint together in the same glass.[173]

RON BACARDÍ JULEP (1915 VERSION)

Proceed as with the "Mint Julep" employing rum in place of Cognac.

However, in the 1935 and 1937 editions of the *Bar La Florida* cocktail book, all of the ingredients come together in both a rum version and a gin version:[174]

MOJITO CRIOLLO (1935 VERSION)

use an 8-ounce glass
Cracked ice
Several sprigs of hierbabuena
1 lemon peel, squeezing juice into glass
1 teaspoon sugar
2 ounces Martí Rum
Stir with spoon. Add sparkling water and serve without straining.[175]

---

173   J.B. Escalante, *Manuel Del Cantinero* (1st edn, Imprénta Moderna 1915) 48

174   *Bar La Florida* (La Florida 1935) 47

175   It is assumed that the recipe calls for the lemon shell to be tossed into the glass.

Similarly, in the 1936 edition of *Sloppy Joe's Cocktails Manual*, the Mojito calls for both mint plus the lime juice and shell.[176]

MOJITO (1936 VERSION)

1 teaspoon sugar
One half a lime
1 part rum
Seltzer Water
Leaves of mint
Shell of the juiced lime
Serve in a highball glass with cracked ice.

Albert Stevens Crockett included a version of the Mojito in the 1935 edition of his *Old Waldorf-Astoria Bar Book*, simply defining it as being a rickey with a little sugar and a few sprigs of mint added.[177]

Over in Britain, the Mojito was included in the supplementary list of drinks whose recipes are not provided in the 1937 *Café Royal Cocktail Book*. In the section's introduction the reader is invited to write to the United Kingdom Bartenders Guild for a copy of the recipe at a cost of 1 shilling per recipe.

La Florida added a Mojito Criollo No. 1 that employed lemon juice and peel to its repertoire.

---

176 *Sloppy Joe's Cocktail Manual* (1st edn, Sloppy Joe's 1936) 9

177 Albert Stevens Crockett, The Old Waldorf-Astoria Bar Book (AS Crockett 1935) 136

MOJITO CRIOLLO NO. 1 (1939 VERSION)

Use an 8-ounce glass
Cracked ice
Several springs of peppermint
1 quarter lemon peel,
squeezing juice into the glass
1 teaspoon sugar
2 ounces Havana Club
Stir with spoon. Add sparkling Canada Dry water and
serve without straining.[178]

By the time Angel Martinez bought out the Bodega La Complaciente on Calle Empedrado, in 1942, and renamed it Casa Martinez, the Mojito in its most familiar form had already evolved, a descendant of the Rum Rickey with the added aroma of mint; born from hands of a bartender at the La Concha Bar, forty years earlier, and modified to suit local palates. By the time he officially "inaugurated" La Bodeguita del Medio on 26 April 1950, he was already well known amongst Havana literati and avant-garde for his version of the drink, thanks to editor Felito Ayon and Ernest Hemingway.

But what of muddling the mint in the drink? Based on a description narrated by Hector Zumbado that was excerpted from *Prosas en Ajiaco*, it appears that La Bodeguita's *cantineros* started that trend. But the lime was squeezed into the glass—not muddled, which imparts too much bitterness into the drink.[179]

Some modern bartenders make the mistake of muddling the mint with lime wedges instead of squeezing in the juice and then dropping in the shell. Additionally, muddling the mint instead of "spanking" it to release the volatile oils does cause the mint to go chalky on the palate.

---

178   Bar La Florida (La Florida 1939) 47

179   Lam

Let's discuss the origins of the word "mojito" which Campoamor cites as a diminutive of the term "mojo". He states that it derives from the sauce that is made in the Canary Islands by the same name. The sauce—which contains garlic, cumin, coriander, chili, avocado, and lemon juice—has little to nothing to do with the cooler made with rum, lime or lemon juice, and in later recipes, mint.[180] Based on an assertion that the term is of African origin does lead us to believe that this diminutive is born from the term "mojo" that refers to a type of magical charm used in hoodoo and Santeria rituals. The mojo "spell" consists of a drawstring bag that is filled with herbs, spices, minerals, an incantation, and other objects that is used to invoke luck, attract love, money, induce confidence, or ward off demons and enemies.[181] A drink that made you feel good could be magical in that respect and would be christened with an endearment such as "dear little spell" in a culture that embraces Santeria such as Cuban culture.

As with the case of the Daiquirí, it is safe to assume that there are two Mojitos. One is based on the Rum Rickey. The other is a variation on a Mint Julep. The two recipes came together during the 1930s at Sloppy Joe's and at El Floridita. Either of these establishments would have been the first to produce the drink that was ultimately popularised, during the 1950s, by Angel Martinez at La Bodeguita del Medio. A survey of Sloppy Joe's drinks menus from 1918 through 1936 would best determine when the bar first started serving Mojitos. Similarly, a survey of La Florida's menus from 1900 through 1936 would determine when the establishment started serving Mojitos Criollos. Based on the Sloppy Joe's and El Floridita recipes, Angel Martinez was the first to muddle the mint according to the Mint Julep fashion.

---

180 Campoamor 139

181 ibid.

What of the La Concha recipe? The La Concha Mojito is an exception to the rule that became the standard for making a Mojito. Thus, it should be considered as a separate and unique recipe on its own. Since we cannot find a copy of any material that proves up the La Concha Mojito recipe from 1910, we cannot verify that it is an authentic recipe.

One thing is certain, though. The Mojito is an authentic "born in Cuba" mixed drink.

Daiquirí: An Identity Crisis in a Glass

The story of the quintessential Rum Sour—the Daiquirí—begins with the overwhelmingly popular beverage that ruled the drinks menu for over 200 years. Punch by all accounts is the ancestor of the Daiquirí. In a 1760 French translation of the 1743 proceedings of the Royal Society of London, Punch—or "the Perfect Fifth"—is described as a compound that contains water, sugar, lemon, and eau-de-vie. But the same document cautions that for use in the autumn and winter, one should eliminate the lemon and increase the sugar and spirit.[182]

---

182   'Transactions Philosophiques De La Société Royale De Londres Pour Le Mois De Février 1743' (1760) 7 *Transactions Philosophiques de la Société Royale de Londres pour le Mois de Février 1743*, 211. The entry reads: "*Le Ponche, ou le Diapente, comme je l'ai appelle improprement, je fait ansi: Prenez deux livres d'eau, une once & demie de sucre, deux onces & demie de juc [sic] de limon récent, trois onces & demie d'eau de vie, mêlez le tout ensemble. C'est le ponche que nous bûvons communément en Eté; mais celui dont nous faison usage en Automne & en Hiver est plus fort, contenant plus de sucre & d'eau de vie, & moins d'acide. C'est une boisson agréeable, acidulée & rafraîchissante; elle fait un excellent diaphorétique dans le temps chaud & un bon diurétique dans un temps froid.* [Ponche or Diapente, as I incorrectly called it. Take two pounds of water, an ounce and a half of sugar, two ounces and a half of juc [sic] of recent silt, three ounces and a half brandy, mix everything together. This is the Ponche [which] we commonly drink in Summer; but the one we make in Autumn and Winter in is stronger, containing more sugar and eau-de-vie, and less acid . It's a nice drink and refreshing acidulous; she is an excellent diaphoretic in the warm weather & a good diuretic in cold weather.]"

PONCHE
AKA: DIAPENTE

16 ounces water
1 ½ ounces sugar
2 ½ ounces fresh lemon juice
3 ½ ounces spirit

Sounds familiar, doesn't it?

In his 1734 dictionary of French, Spanish, and Latin, author Francisco Sobrino defined *ponche* as a British drink made from aguardiente, water, lemon, and sugar: *PONCHE, s.s. Ponche, bebida Inglesa, que le hace de aguardiente, agua, limon y azucar.*[183]

Is it possible that the British introduced Punch to Cuba?

British East India Company seamen, freebooters, and adventurers travelling the Indian Ocean in the early 1600s quickly adopted Punch (derived from *panch*, the Hindi term for the number "five"). Made from five ingredients: sugar, lemon, water, tea, and arrack, this libation lured the sipper with the exotic tastes of citrus, sugar, and tea that they had otherwise not experienced in seventeenth-century Europe.

It is likely that the citrus juice coupled with the addictive sweetness of sugar made this drink irresistible to scurvy-prone, vitamin-C-deficient sailors.

In the West Indies, one would be pretty hard pressed to find a local source for tea. Already popular at home, it was no surprise that seamen crafted a rum version. Captain William Dampier mentioned how widespread this "punch" was in his 1699 memoirs, commenting that while he was on the island of Tortuga he noticed that: "Ships

---

183   Francisco Sobrino, *Nouveau Dictionnaire De Sobrino, François, Espagnol Et Latin, III* (1st edn, Delamolliere 1791) 381

coming from some of the Caribbean islands are always well stored with Rum, Sugar, and Lime-juice to make Punch, to hearten their Men when they are at work getting and bringing aboard the Salt…"[184]

The tradition of providing regular sailors with a daily tot of rum had long been established within the British Royal Navy when rum was decreed, by 1687, an official part of sailors' daily rations.[185] The British Royal Navy's vice-Admiral Edward "Old Grog" Vernon issued Order to Captains No. 349 on 21 August 1740 that the daily rum ration should be: "…every day mixed with the proportion of a quart of water to a half pint of rum, to be mixed in a scuttled butt kept for that purpose, and to be done upon the deck, and in the presence of the Lieutenant of the Watch who is to take particular care to see that the men are not defrauded in having their full allowance of rum… and let those that are good husband men receive extra lime juice and sugar that to be made more palatable to them."[186]

During the Seven Years' War (1754-1763) the British Royal Navy captured the Spanish colonial city of Havana in the 1762 Battle of Havana that lasted from March through August. This would have been enough time for a certain amount of British influence to enter the Cuban cultural fabric. But there is also evidence of a local concoction made from the same or similar ingredients.

A simple compound of honey, aguardiente and lemon juice named Canchánchara is believed by some historians to have been invented during the Ten Years War (1868-1878) in Trinidad, Cuba. Others say that it was born in the eastern part of the island.

---

184   William Dampier and Albert Gray, *A New Voyage Round The World* (James Knapton 1699).

185   *Regulations And Instructions Relating To His Majesty's Service At Sea.* (1734) 62

186   Vernon was nicknamed "Old Grog" because of his waterproof grogam coat made from gum-stiffened silk, wool, and mohair that he wore on deck.

CANCHÁNCHARA

60 ml aguardiente
2 spoonfuls honey
1 teaspoon lemon juice
Ice
Mix well in a glass the honey
and lime juice. Add aguardiente
and ice. Stir.[187]

During the 1800s the drink may not have necessarily been made with rum, but with aguardiente de caña, which was cheaper and equally abundant. But was honey the original sweetener? *Miel*—being another term for the molasses used in rum production—could be just that. Molasses, not honey.

Yet the *New York Herald* special commissioner AB Henderson we mentioned earlier did speak of a Cuba Libre made from "hot water" [read: aguardiente de caña] and honey. Later, the 1902 book *Farrow & Jackson Limited's Recipes for American and Other Iced Drinks* documented the existence of a drink called Rum & Honey.

Because of its unique location in the Caribbean, Cuba is blessed with abundant and varied flowers, making honey from this island more aromatic and complex in character than single-flowered varieties. It is produced throughout the island.

The healthful properties of Cuban honey combined with rum are told on the El Floridita web site, narrating that: "The combination of two thirds of rum and one third of lemon juice was an efficient cure for the thirst of the Cuban combatants fighting against the Spanish colonial army during the second part of the 19th century. It was an excellent painkiller for the injured persons. This is why a bottle of Canchánchara was often seeing hung at the saddle of the

---

187 'Canchánchara' (Es.wikipedia.org, 2008) <http://es.wikipedia.org/wiki/Canchanchara> accessed 23 October 2008.

soldiers' mount. From that time, it has been a synonym of the struggle of the Cuban people for their independence."[188]

On the same web site, El Floridita narrates a story about the birth of the Daiquirí that connects it to Canchánchara: "In 1898 the American troops, under the command of General Shafter, landed in the south-east region of the Daiquirí area..... In spite of his faults, he was an inveterate gourmet. He didn't take long time to discover the preferred drink of Cuban patriots, a mixture of rum, lemon juice and sugar. Tasting it he declared: 'Only one ingredient is missing: ice'."[189]

It is possible that the same compound called Cuba Libre—as titled by American journalists who misinterpreted "hot water and honey" from "burning water and honey"—may have also contained citrus juice. Cuba Libre may have been the alternate name given to Canchánchara by non-Spanish speakers. As a "native" compound, it is also possible that the elements inspired the creation of the Daiquirí by an American engineer who had close associations with the Cuban Liberation Army.

The most commonly distributed story about the Daiquirí's birth involves an 1898 meeting between Jennings Stockton Cox Jr and Francesco Domenico Pagliuchi.

New York mining engineer Jennings S Cox Jr was the general manager of the Spanish-American Iron Company, starting in 1896, and a member of the American Institute of Mining Engineers. A fellow member of the association, Francesco Domenico Pagliuchi was also an engineer. Additionally, he was a war correspondent for *Harper's Monthly* as well as a commander in the Liberating Army of Cuba. He wrote an account of a nighttime supply landing at Daiquirí titled "How a Filibustering Expedition Was Landed" amongst other

---

188   'Daiquiri' (El Floridita, 2008) <http://www.elfloridita.net/pages/Daiquirí. php?language=en> accessed 23 October 2008.n

189   ibid.

reports. The story narrates how his own troop of upper-class Cuban civilians managed to land essential supplies from off-shore American supply vessels.[190]

When bartender Emilio "Maragato" González, who was famous for popularising the Daiquirí in Havana passed away on 30 July 1940, it was Pagliuchi who corrected the details of the drink's invention. Apparently, the editor of *El Pais* newspaper made a glaring error in writing Maragato's obituary, crediting the bartender with the Daiquirí's origination. Pagliuchi sent the following correction: "In today's edition of your appreciable periodical 'El Pais' I have read an article titled, 'There died yesterday evening 'Maragato', the inventor of 'Daiquirí.' Allow me to clarify that the delicious 'Daiquirí' was not invented in Havana, but in the mines of Daiquirí, by the Engineer [Jennings S] Cox[Jr], the director of these mines."

"At the conclusion of the war of independence of Cuba [in 1898], in which I had very active part, I obtained American capital to reactivate the old El Cobre copper mines situated near Santiago de Cuba, of which I was the director. While occupied in this work, I had occasion to go to Daiquirí to speak with mister Cox. Concluding the matter that I took to Daiquirí, I asked mister Cox if he was going to invite me for a cocktail."[191]

"In the sideboard of the mine's dining room, there was not gin nor vermouth; there was only Bacardí, lemons, sugar, and ice. With these elements we did a very well shaken and very cold cocktail that I liked much. Then I asked Cox: — and this: how is it called? He answered: 'Rum Sour'. In the United States there is a drink that is called a 'Whisky Sour', which is made with whisky, sugar, lemon

190   F.D. Pagliuchi, 'How A Filibustering Expedition Was Landed' [1898] *Harper's Pictoral History of the War with Spain* 123-124

191   H.A. Sanchez, *El Arte Del Cantinero O Los Vinos Y Los Licores.* (1st edn, P Fernandez y Cia 1948). 275

juice and ice". But I said to him: 'This name is very long, why not call it Daiquirí?'"[192]

In his food and drink travelogue, *The Gentleman's Companion*, Charles H Baker Jr added a friend of his to this cast of characters: "The 2 originators were my friend Harry E Stout, now domiciled in Englewood, New Jersey, and a mining engineer associate, Mr Jennings Cox. TIME: summer of 1898. PLACE: Daiquirí..."[193]

ORIGINAL CUBAN DAIQUIRÍ (BAKER VERSION)

1 whiskey glass (1 ½ oz) level full of Carta Blanca, or Carta de Oro Bacardi rum,
2 tsp of sugar,
the juice of 1 ½ small green limes
—strained; and very
finely cracked ice.[194]

There was no Harry E Stout. But there was a Henry E Stout. According to his 1918 USA passport application, Henry Eugene Stout resided outside of the United States living in Port Limon, Costa Rica (from 1901 to 1903), Yucatan, Mexico (1904 to 1905), and Felton, Cuba (1911 to October 1916). He listed his permanent address as Camagüey, Cuba, where he was the general shop foreman for the Cuba Railroad, an American Corporation.[195] At the time of his 1918 application, he had retired from his job as a mechanic and

---

192   Sanchez 275

193   Charles H. Baker, Jr., The Gentleman's Companion: Volume II, Being An Exotic Drinking Book Or, Around The Word With Jigger, Beaker And Flask (1st edn, Derrydale Press 1939) 30-31

194   ibid.

195   Department Passport Application 28483. National Archives and Records Administration (NARA); Washington D.C.; Passport Applications, January 2, 1906 - March 31, 1925; Collection Number: ARC Identifier 583830 / MLR Number A1 534; NARA Series: M1490; Roll #: 560.

planned to visit relatives living in Audubon, New Jersey.[196] Thus, he was not an engineer as described by Baker. It is possible that before he moved to Costa Rica, he travelled to Cuba. But there is no record of him on any passenger lists sailing from the USA.

Based on Pagliuchi's letter to the editor, the recipe for a Daiquirí— or Rum Sour— was similar to a Whiskey Sour or a Medford Rum Sour recipe from the same period:

WHISKEY SOUR

1/2 tablespoonful of sugar;
3 or 4 dashes of lemon juice;
1 squirt of syphon selter water,
dissolve the sugar and lemon well
with a spoon
Fill the glass with ice;
1 wine glass of whiskey:
Stir up well, strain into a sour glass;
Place your fruit into it, and serve.[197]

MEDFORD RUM SOUR

(use a large bar glass.)
1/2 tablespoonful of sugar;
3 or 4 dashes of lemon juice;
1 squirt of syphon selter, dissolved well
1 wine glass of Medford rum;
Fill 1/2 of the glass with ice.
Stir well with a spoon strain
into a sour glass, ornament with fruit,
etc., and serve.
This is an old Boston drink, and has the reputation of
being cooling and pleasant.[198]

196   US Department Passport Application 28483

197   Johnson 184

198   Johnson 209

Another version that did not include a squirt of soda water called a Columbia Skin came even closer to the Daiquirí formula:

COLUMBIA SKIN
1 teaspoonful sugar,
dissolve with a little water;
1 slice of lemon;
2 or 3 pieces of broken ice;
1 wine glass of Medford rum;
Stir up well with a spoon;
grate a little nutmeg on top and serve.
This drink is called Columbia Skin
by the Boston people.[199]

In all of these recipes, the Sour was stirred. Does this means that the "original" Daiquirí was not a shaken drink, but a stirred compound? Not necessarily. Both methods were employed in making Sours during the period.

So the Daiquirí—in American eyes—was simply a Rum Sour made with Cuban rum instead of the more familiar New England distilled rums which were more popular in the American market.

Pagliuchi's correction of the *El País* obituary about Emilio "Maragato" González provides strong evidence that there was more than one Daiquirí receiving global praise. His beloved Cox Daiquirí was made with lemons and mixed according to a classic Sour recipe. The other Daiquirí, the Bacardí Daiquirí used limes and offered a grenadine option.

Pagliuchi's defence of the Cox Daiquirí means that the story surrounding the Daiquirí served by Maragato might have followed the Bacardí Daiquirí recipe. But he felt strongly enough about the subject to write to the editor even though he had emigrated to the USA

199   Johnson 209

by 1905 via London and travelled frequently to Venezuela until he relocated from New York to Los Angeles.[200]

Another version of the Jennings S Cox Jr story was circulated in the *Miami Herald*, in 1937, by Facundo M Bacardí, one of Don Facundo Bacardí y Massó's younger sons.[201] However, this recipe that allegedly originated at the Venus Bar in Santiago de Cuba is a carbon copy of La Florida's frappéed speciality, having little to do with Pagliuchi's version.[202] In the same breath, he also attributes the recipe blessed by him to the work of the Sevilla-Biltmore's Eddie Woelke.[203] Since a similar recipe appears in Jacques Straub 1914 book *Drinks*, it makes the tale even more myth than truth.

Amongst the men who have been listed as being present at the naming of this drink by various sources are J Francis Linthicum, C Manning Combs, George W Pfeiffer, De Berneire Whitaker, C Merritt Holmes, and Proctor O Persing.[204] No mention is made of either Francesco Domenico Pagliuchi nor of Charles H Baker Jr's friend Henry Eugene Stout. All of these men could have been in the Daiquirí area, but it is difficult to say if they were present, especially De Bernier Whitaker and C Merritt Holmes, whose names do not appear on any passenger lists for people sailing to or from Cuba during that period.

The person of most interest is Proctor O Persing, age 33, who sailed on 15 September 1911 from Santiago de Cuba on the SS *Prinz August Wilhelm* bound for New York. This one voyage carried two other passengers: a student named Facundo Bacardí, age 21, and

---

200   Form for Naturalized Citizen, No. 77735, 17 December 1917.

201   The Miami Herald, 'Origin Is Disclosed Of Daiquiri Cocktail: One Of Group Of American Engineers Named The Drink At Santiago Bar' (1937)

202   ibid.

203   ibid.

204   'Daiquiri' (El Floridita, 2008) <http://www.elfloridita.net/pages/Daiquirí.php?language=en> accessed 23 October 2008.

Arturo Schueg, age 15, who was son of Henri Schueg, Emilio Bacardí's brother-in-law and the man who was eventually became responsible for the company's international marketing strategy.[205]

The young Bacardí possibly heard the tale from the older Proctor
Persing whilst sailing to New York. More than likely the Venus Hotel Bar crafted a version that resonated with its patrons including
Persing. These drinks may have contained the same ingredients, but
by execution were not from the Sour family of compounds described
by Pagliuchi.

A more recent version of the story that has circulated in print and on
the internet includes a hand-written version of the recipe that was pur-
portedly produced by Jennings S Cox Jr and handed out to patrons.

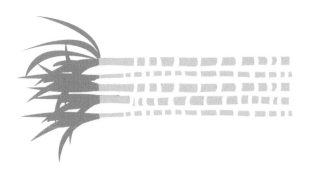

DAIQUIRÍ ("MR COX" VERSION)
(for 6 persons)
The juice of 6 lemons
6 teaspoons of sugar
6 Bacardí cups— "Carta Blanca"
2 small cups of mineral water
Plenty of crushed ice
Put all ingredients in a cocktail
shaker and shake well. Do not strain
as the glass may be served with
some ice. [206]

The writing in the upper right corner is curious. If this was hand-
written and distributed by Cox, why does it say "original" and "Mr
Cox's"?[207] This is not a usual statement of first- person authorship.
According to the Diffords-Guide database, this recipe allegedly

205   Year: 1911; Arrival: New York, New York; Microfilm Serial: T715, 1897-1957; Microfilm Roll: Roll 1742; Line: 23; Page Number: 175

206   "Daiquiri". Retrieved on 27 October 2008 from http://www.havanaturbahamas.
com/drinks.html

207   The image above of the "original Cox's recipe" has appeared throughout the internet blogs ever since National Daiquirí Day (July 19) was announced in 2006 by Bacardí's

came from Jennings Cox Jr's personal diary.[208] But if this piece paper came from his personal diary, why does "Original Mr Cox" appear in the corner of what is obviously an index card.

But then that entry also states that: "US Admiral Lucius Johnson fought in the Spanish-American War." That fact will be played out later as being false. Another problem with Difford's entry is the mention that "Cox's granddaughter recounts a slightly different tale; namely that Cox ran out of gin when entertaining American guests. Wary of serving them straight rum, he added lime and sugar."

When Jennings and Isabel Cox sailed to New York on 2 May 1913 on board the SS *Prinz Joachim*, the 46- and 44-year-old couple was not accompanied by any children.[209] Even in his 1913 obituary, Cox was survived by only his father and his wife.[210] The story attached to this "discovered" piece of evidence obviously has a few flaws. Namely, without children, how would Cox have had a granddaughter?

However, this Daiquirí recipe does agree with Pagliuchi's account that uses lemons, not limes or key limes.

A journalist for the *New York Sun* newspaper, G Selmer Fougner, compiled and published material, in 1935, for his "Along the Wine Trail" columns into a book. Hoping to educate a new generation of post-Prohibition drinkers who knew nothing of the history of

---

public relations agency of record, Corbin & Associates Limited, who took over the brand from the Baddish Group, the agency responsible for promoting the Mojito during the 1990s. Although this is not a government-sanctioned nor presidential-decreed national day such as National ice Cream, which also takes place on the third Sunday of July, the PR agency has continued promoting the "original" Daiquirí using this image.

208   "Daiquirí No. 1 Natural (Difford's 10:3:2 recipe)" in Difford's Guide. Retrieved on 3 February 2011 from http://www.diffordsguide.com/site/main/welcome.jsp?cocktail-Id=611

209   Year: 1913; Arrival: New York, New York; Microfilm Serial: T715, 1897-1957; Microfilm Roll: Roll 2073; Line: 1; Page Number: 12

210   The New York Times, 'Obituaries: Jennings S Cox Jr' (1913)

distillation and popular drinks, Fougner [*see left*] detailed numerous "lost" cocktails.

Of the Daiquirí Fougner wrote: "Jennings S Cox, inventor of the famous Daiquirí, was strongly opposed to called the drink a 'cocktail.' From long years spent in Cuba, he held strongly to the theory that the wise traveller should, so far as possible, confine himself to the food and drink native to the country in which he chanced to be. And the Daiquirí, for that reason was, in his opinion, the ideal Cuban drink." Meticulous in its preparation, Cox thoroughly mixed one of lime, two of sugar, and three of rum which was poured over finely cracked ice packed in a coupette.[211]

If we are to believe Fougner's statement about Cox's desire to eat and drink native recipes, then the compass points true in the relationship between the Canchánchara and the Daiquirí.

Remember the 1937 *Miami Herald* article about the origins of the Daiquirí that was previously mentioned? There are two fascinating statements at the end of that reporter's piece: "During prohibition this drink was pitifully abused. Many establishments used grenadine in place of sugar, and this still obtains today. There is a cocktail called Santiago which requires no sweetening, but is absolutely

---

211   G.S. Fougner, *Along The Wine Trail: An Anthology Of Wines And Spirits* (The Stratford Company 1935).

wrong to give it the name Daiquirí. ...The Daiquirí and Bacardí cocktails are the same."[212]

The Bacardí Cocktail was so popular after Prohibition's repeal it was served along with Daiquirí everywhere and not always made with Bacardí, even at the hotel where the company's sales marketing director Fausto Rodriguez resided in 1936, the Barbizon-Plaza Hotel in New York's Upper East Side. A 1936 decision by the appellate division of the New York Supreme Court that a Bacardí cocktail must be made with the namesake brand.[213] Yet, New York Supreme Court Justice Rosenman ruled against the company's claim against the hotel, stating that "The plaintiff does not show sufficient clearness to warrant a temporary injunction...."[214] This was not the first or only case of its kind.

Heublein sued the Adams Company in Massachusetts, in 1903, and successfully in US Supreme Court in 1904 for infringing on its Club Cocktails trademarked name.[215]

Ironically, when the free bar opened in the Bacardí Building in Havana, in 1931, American journalists were treated to a Daiquirí (touted as the national drink).[216]

Was it that consumers lost their sweet tooth and didn't favour the use of grenadine any longer? Possibly.

Nevertheless, an attempt to trademark the name "Daiquirí Bacardí" in the USA for a "liquor with a rum base known generically as

212   The Miami Herald, 'Origin Is Disclosed Of Daiquiri Cocktail: One Of Group Of American Engineers Named The Drink At Santiago Bar' (1937)

213   A Benes, 'Spirit Of The Bat: The Rum Dynasty: Bacardí' [1996] *Cigar Aficionado*

214   The New York Times, 'LOSES COCKTAIL SUIT: Bacardí Firm Fails To Prove Use Of Its Rum Is Essential' (1936)

215   Heublein v Adams [1904] CCMass, 125 Fed 785 (CCMass)

216   San Antonio Light, 'Another Free Bar In Havana' (1934).

'Daiquirí" was opposed, on 22 January 1935, by Compania Ron Daiquirí SV of Havana.[217] At the time, Ron Daiquirí was making headway, exporting its product to the US and Britain, where it was being adopted by key influencers such as the Savoy's Harry Craddock and UKBG President William J Tarling.[218]

KING'S JUBILEE
Invented by Harry Craddock
¼ Lemon Juice.
¼ Luxardo's Maraschino (Dry).
½ Daiquiri Rum.
Shake and strain into cocktail glass.[219]

CUBAN MANHATTAN
½ Daiquiri Rum.
½ Martini Sweet Vermouth
2 dashes Angostura Bitters.[220]

DAIQUIRÍ (1937 VERSION)
3 dashes Gomme Syrup.
¾ Daiquiri Rum.
¼ Juice of a Lime or Lemon.
Shake.[221]

---

217   'Decision Of The Commissioner Of Patents: Descriptive Terms' (The Trademark Reporter 1935)

218   It is interesting to note that Tarling's 1937 book *Café Royal Cocktail Book* presented 49 recipes that contain Daiquiri Rum

219   Tarling 117

220   Tarling 61

221   Tarling 62

DAIQUIRI BLOSSOM
½ Orange Juice.
½ Daiquiri Rum.
1 dash Maraschino.
Shake and strain.[222]

DAIQUIRI GRAPEFRUIT BLOSSOM
1/3 Grapefruit Juice.
2/3 Daiquiri Rum.
3 dashes Maraschino.
Shake and strain.[223]

DAIQUIRI LIBERAL
2/3 Daiquiri Rum.
1/3 Martini Sweet Vermouth.
1 dash Amer Picon.
Use mixing glass.[224]

DAIQUIRI OLD-FASHIONED
1 dash Angostura Bitters.
2 dashes Orange Bitters.
1 lump of Sugar dissolved in
two spoonsful of Water.
1 glass Daiquiri Rum.
Serve in an old-fashioned glass
and serve with fruit and mint.[225]

222 Tarling 63

223 ibid.

224 ibid.

225 ibid.

DAIQUIRI SPECIAL
1 teaspoonful Grenadine.
1/3 Gin.
2/3 Daiquiri Rum
The Juice of ½ Lime
Shake and strain into cocktail glass.[226]

FAIR & WARMER
1/3 Italian Vermouth.
2/3 Daiquiri Rum.
2 dashes Curasao [sic].
Mix and strain into cocktail glass.[227]

The alleged landmark lawsuit had more to do with the fact that if Compania Ron Daiquirí could stop them from using the word "Daiquirí" coupled with Bacardí, then they could stop anyone from making a Bacardí Cocktail without Bacardí!

However, the conflict may not have started in the USA. It may have first erupted in Havana.

With the promotional push in Havana of the Daiquirí by Bacardí, the José Arechabala S.A.'s Havana Club brand chose a different name for its version of the Daiquirí when in 1934 it opened its "private club bar". The company publicised its Havana Club Special "Frozen Cocktail" on its complimentary admission cards.

---

226   Tarling 64

227   Tarling 75

HAVANA CLUB SPECIAL

1 tsp sugar
½ oz lime or lemon juice
1 oz Havana Club Rum
Dissolve lime juice and sugar first
in the cocktail shaker. Add Havana
Club Rum and cracked ice according
to number of cocktails to be mixed.
Shake this mixture until it is frozen.

Lemon or lime juice was suggested in the recipe. This was smart marketing on the part of Havana Club, especially since Compania Ron Daiquirí had its sights set on suing Bacardí for infringement of the name Daiquirí.

Why was there an option for lemon or lime juice?

Americans living in the Midwest and the North were not accustomed to the taste of limes. Until the late twentieth century, limes were hard to come by in those regions; had a limited growing season even in Florida; and were not a familiar taste.

Emilio "Maragato" González was famed for his Daiquirís which he served around 1913 at the Hotel Plaza, according to Jaime Ariansen Cespedes which were probably made with lime or key lime juice.[228]

However, it was the version that La Florida's owner, Constantino Ribalaigua Vert, created—the Daiquirí Frappé (aka: Daiquirí No. 4)—that became the toast of the town and the entire world.

Jack Cuddy mentions a medium *lima* [lime]. But the recipes that followed in the same book dictated that Constante's five versions of the Daiquirí used *limon verde* [green lemon] which the English translator interpreted as lemon.

228 'La Historia Del Daiquirí: El Ciclón Del Caribe' (2012) <http://www. historiacocina. com/historia/articulos/Daiquirí.htm> accessed 2 February 2012

We won't discuss the obvious facts about the El Floridita Daiquirís. Thanks to author Ernest Hemingway, it is the Daiquirí #4 that has the longest legs. It resonated with the A-list celebrity set to whom Hemingway introduced both the bar and the drink, for the most part, until he left Cuba.

Bottom line: No one ever seemed to get the recipes for the Daiquirí and the Bacardí cocktails right. Even by 1960, two conflicting recipes for the Bacardí cocktail appear in the United Kingdom Bartenders' Guide official drink guide—the book that was supposed to standardise recipes throughout its membership.

The truth is, there is more than one drink that was christened Daiquirí and there always has been. In many ways it is much like the story of the two Blackthorn Cocktails, one made with Irish whiskey, the other made with Sloe Gin.

It's also like the story of the two Mai Tais, a short drink created by Trader Vic Bergeron and a long drink created by Ernst Beaumont Gantt of Don the Beachcomber. A great name that resonates with consumers is hard to beat.

There are three drinks named the Daiquirí which are progressive, stylistic modifications to the British Ponche and the Cuban Canchánchara formula of rum, citrus juice, sweetener, and dilution:

- Jennings S Cox's Daiquirí that follows the classic Rum Sour recipe: rum, lemon juice, mineral water, and sugar.

- Facundo Bacardí's Daiquirí: rum, lime juice, and sugar with the option to add grenadine syrup.

- Constante Ribalaigua's Daiquirí #4 (aka: El Floridita Daiquirí): rum, lime juice, maraschino liqueur, and sugar.

Variations on these three recipes abound between 1900 and 1979, varying the citrus to sweetness levels.

So then which was the original recipe? All of them. It depends on your personal preference.

Cuba Libre: From Rum & Honey to Rum & Cola

Cuba Libre. The phrase *was* most closely associated with the Ten Years' War 1868-1878— not with the Spanish-American War—when the world media first took note of the island nation's fight for independence. But few people realise that it was also linked to a beverage, according to the *New York Herald*'s special commissioner who followed the freedom fighters to the battlefield at Viamones:[229] The repast consisted of one dish—roast beef—and nothing else, and in the way of liquids we were invited to hot water, sweetened with honey—a concoction known as "Cuba Libre".

The commissioner had encountered the drink a month earlier when he met up with a "picket guard" of 108 fighters on his way to General Manuel Agramonte's headquarters: "They have meat, with vegetables and oranges and lemons in abundance, but no coffee. Their beverage is hot water, sweetened with honey, which they call Cuba libre.[230]

There are some obvious questions that arise about the ingredients of this Cuba Libre. This newspaperman—as well as others sent to report from the battlefields—surely relied on translators to aid him

229 The New York Herald, 'CUBA. Report Of The Herald Commissioner, Mr. AB Henderson' (1872)

230 The New York Herald, 'INSURGENT CUBA. Herald Special Report From The Seat Of Insurrection' (1872)

in communicating with the revolutionary forces. Therefore it is very difficult to say if this Cuba Libre was made with hot water or "burning water" (read: aguardiente).

Were the freedom fighters actually drinking rum with honey? Were they drinking Canchánchara, which was later known as the revolutionaries' drink of choice in the jungle?

One other term comes into question. The molasses used to make rum also goes by the same term as honey: *miel,* in Latin American Spanish. So it is hard to say if these American corespondents encountered a hot molasses beverage or a hot honey beverage.

Wouldn't it be ironic if the original Cuba Libre was the Canchánchara, a drink we discussed earlier?

There was a rum and honey beverage that, in 1902, made it into British drinks books that leads one to wonder if this Cuba Libre, this Canchánchara, was exported as Cuban rum took its first steps off the island:

122—RUM AND HONEY. S.D.
Take a wine glass; put in a small piece of ice; and a teaspoonful of Bourbon honey; fill up glass with "Liquid Sunshine" rum; stir well with spoon and place slice of lemon of [SIC] top.[231]

The phrase "Cuba Libre" was firmly ensconced, by 1898, in the American newspaper vernacular and thus in popular language as evidenced when the headquarters for the VII Army Corps under

---

231   C. Paul, *Farrow & Jackson Limited'S Recipes Of American And Other Iced Drinks* (Farrow & Jackson 1902)

the command of General Fitzhugh Lee in Jacksonville, Florida, was christened with that same name.

American public opinion about Cuba revved up to a fever pitch. Memories of the reports published during the Ten Years' War (1868-1878) were coupled with a constant flow of headlines about the atrocities inflicted by Spanish forces upon Cubans.

Then the mysterious sinking of the American battleship *USS Maine* in Havana harbour, on 15 February 1898, struck the final, tender nerve, especially when newspaper publishers William Randolph Hearst and Joseph Pulitzer used the incident as the perfect ploy to increase sales. The outcry to free America's island neighbour from Spanish rule—perpetrated by the headlines seen in Hearst's *The New York Journal* and Pulitzer's *New York World*— exemplify the power which "yellow journalism" wielded in swaying the public through the misleading headlines and sensationalised reportage, accentuated with lurid illustrations.

The cry of "Cuba Libre!" resounded throughout the US as news syndicates picked up the stories from Bangor, Maine to San Diego, California. Political pressure then forced US President William McKinley's administration to declare war on Spain. (The Teller Amendment, enacted on 20 April 1898, stipulated that as a result in its involvement in war, the US could not annex Cuba, but had to leave control of the island to its people.)

The Spanish-American War began on 23 April 1898 with its official declaration. The US Navy was sent in to create a sea blockade. Then 3000 American troops and volunteers led by General William R Shafter [*see right*] landed in Daiquirí and Siboney that June to support the approximate 30,000 Cuban freedom fighters.

A little over a month later, the American invasion force pulled up stakes and departed the island.[232]

Spain sued for peace after debilitating defeats in Cuba and the Philippines. The fighting ended on 12 August 1898 with the signing of the Protocol for Peace.[233] (The final and formal Treaty of Paris was signed on 10 December 1898.[234])

An American flag was raised on Morro Castle in Havana. US President William McKinley ordered, on New Year's Day 1899, the establishment of a provisional military government headed by General John R Brooke as, on 11 April 1899, the conditions of the treaty came into full force. And so ended the passionate association between the phrase "Cuba Libre" and the freedom fighters' beverage.

A new chapter began when the name was affixed to another rum drink for just a glimmer in time.

Atlanta drugstore owner and patent medicine manufacturer Asa Griggs Candler had purchased, in 1887, from John Pemberton the formula for the non-alcoholic version of Pemberton's kola nut and coca wine tonic, Coca-Cola. An aggressive marketer, Asa was determined to make his new venture a global enterprise. While the final peace treaty between the US and Spain was still in negotiation, his brother Bishop Warren Candler sailed for Cuba to determine what missionary work could be done there. Being a major stockholder in

---

232   Vincent J Cirillo, Bullets And Bacilli (Rutgers University Press 2004). This reason this regiment seemed to evade the outbreak was because these volunteers were mostly African-Americans who had been born and raised in the southern US, where yellow fever was common. Thus many of the men had a natural immunity to the disease.

233   US Government Printing Office, 'The Statutes At Large Of The United States Of America From March 1897 To March 1899 And Recent Treaties, Conventions, Executive Proclamations, And The Concurrent Resolutions Of The Two Houses Of Congress, Volume XXX' (Library of Congress, Asian Division 1899)

234   D. Healy, The United States In Cuba, 1898–1902: Generals, Politicians, And The Search For Policy (University of Wisconsin Press 1963)

his brother's company, the bishop also noted in a letter to Asa that: "We may be sure that commercial currents will follow the channels which education opens and deepens... Here in our duty and our interest coincide."[235]

The wheels were set into motion immediately after the ink dried on the Treaty of Paris and the US took formal possession of Cuba.

Asa Candler enlisted wine merchant José Parejo, in May 1899, to become the Havana-based wholesaler for Coca-Cola. The product was not exported to Cuba until Candler was assured, with American military presence in Cuba, that his investment was safe.

Continued American military presence and an influx of tourism from the US mainland boosted sales while Candler expanded his marketing on a global scale. During the 1920s, the Coca-Cola Company assigned the Cuban production operations to its Canadian branch.

There are some historians who have said that the Cuba Libre was invented, in 1902, at La Florida to celebrate the election of Cuba's first president Tomás Estrada Palma, on 20 May 1902, and its release from American occupation. But the drink does not appear in the 1936 *Bar Florida* book, which provides some evidence that the drink did not originate there.

But H L Mencken, in his 1921 edition of *American Language*, alludes to the fact that in the southern United States, people were already mixing Coca-Cola with spirits, especially ones as cheap as Cuban and Puerto Rican rums were prior to Prohibition.

Basil Woon mentioned the presence of this Cuba Libre highball in Havana's American Club: "Francis Quinlan, his partner. Also

---

235   Mark Pendergrast, *For God, Country, And Coca-Cola* (Scribner's 1993)

a General Motors man. Sometimes plays poker at American Club. Clever at business. Takes his "Cuba Libre" only occasionally."[236]

The American Club, founded in 1902, was a private social club situated at Prado 309, a block from Parque Central. Was it that the bartender at the American Club responded to the whims of his American customers? Or was it that those club members imported a taste for that drink from other place?

Coca-Cola was new to Jamaica, around 1900, when the first export shipment arrived. But the company already had plenty of well-established native competition. Kola wine, kola bitters, kola champagne were all being made locally.[237] Eventually, its popularity led to bottled exports being presented at London's 1905 Crystal Palace.[238]

This leads to the belief that the taste for rum and kola champagne inspired experimentation with rum and Coca-Cola amongst Corps of Army Engineer officers and other members of the American armed forces who encountered the drink in Jamaica. Americans had thoroughly embraced Highballs during the late 1800s, especially the Rickey.

Let's get this straight. The Cuba Libre was not the only drink made of rum, lime, and Coca-Cola. A few versions were promoted during the 1930s. The Puerto Rico Distilling Company marketed its own version—the Carioca Cooler—lauding it as the "Smartest Summer Drink" in the 3 August 1935 edition of *The New Yorker* [*see opposite*].[239]

236   Woon. The entry is footnoted: "Cuba Libre: a highball contrived of coca-cola and Bacardí rum."

237   The Daily Gleaner, 'The Future Of Kola' (1892) 4

238   The Daily Gleaner, 'Jamaica At The Crystal Palace' (1905)

239   'Smartest Summer Drink' [1935] *The New Yorker*

CARIOCA COOLER

1 jigger Rum Carioca
1/2 Lemon or Lime
Coca-Cola
Squeeze lemon or lime into a collins glass.
Drop in the half. Build rum and cola.
Add ice and a straw.

It must have been a very effective promotion, given its national distribution. But it also seems to have caused a good deal of controversy, leading to a court case concerning the association between the Carioca Rum Company and the Coca-Cola Bottling Company. [240]

Either the Coca Cola Company decided to abandon a relationship with the American Spirits Company or never had one. But the campaign disappeared from circulation by the time Lord Invader's (aka: Rupert Grant) and Lionel Belasco's song "Rum and Coca Cola" hit the top of the 1945 US pop singles charts. Recorded by the Andrews Sisters with lyrics reworked by entertainer Morey Amsterdam, the tune brought both Rum & Cola-Cola as well as Cuba Libre to the American public.

The name and the recipe were bantered about in syndicated columns, novels, and cocktail books. From such noted drinks experts as Charles H Baker Jr., Albert Stevens Crockett, Lawrence Blochman, and David Embury made certain both drinks made appearances in their writings. Naturally, Vic Bergeron's 1947 book *Bartender's*

---

240 Carioca Rum Company v Coca-Cola Company [1940] Court of Customs and Patent Appeals, Volume 28 (Court of Customs and Patent Appeals) 1153.

Guide... by Trader Vic includes a Cuba Libre even though his 1946 book *Trader Vic's Food & Drink* does not. But what is more curious is that Bergeron also crafted a Cuba Libre Cocktail recipe with an amazingly different profile.

CUBA LIBRE COCKTAIL (TRADER VIC VERSION)

1 oz Cuban rum
1 oz Coca-Cola Juice
1/2 lime
Shake with cracked ice;
strain into cocktail glass.[241]

It was journalist Lucius Beebe who in his 1946 *The Stork Club Bar Book* provided the key as to why Cuban drinks like the Cuba Libre had become popular. Aggressive advertising and promotion coupled with competitively cheap pricing were the primary causes for Cuban rum's success stateside.[242]

The hidden secret was the "feminine factor in public drinking, since it is universally acknowledged that the thin consistency combined with special suitability of Cuban type rums for mixing with fruits and sugar have a strong appeal to women's taste."[243] This single element alone continues to drive contemporary drink trends as witnessed by the overwhelmingly appeal of Cosmopolitans, Appletinis, and the revival of Tiki drinks even to this day.

So what's our take on the Cuba Libre?

Prior to the 1898 Spanish-American War, there was a drink consumed by Cuban freedom fighters that was called a Cuba Libre in the American press. But it did not contain a cola drink.

---

241   Trader Vic 213

242   Lucius Beebe, *The Stork Club Bar Book* (1st edn, Rinehart & Co 1946) 55-56

243   Beebe 55

The Cuba Libre does not appear in any Cuban cocktail book that was published between the 1900s through 1950s including the 1927 *El Arte de Hacer un Cocktail y Algo Más* and the 1948 *El Arte del Cantineros*. Although it is mentioned as a drink consumed in 1928 by an American executive who was a member of the American Club in Havana, the rum-and-cola Cuba Libre does not make an appearance in print until 1935 in the USA. It appears that lime juice became a standard in the recipe after the 1930s promotional campaign for the Carioca Cooler brought it to prominence.

Although some sources make the distinction between Cuba Libre and Rum & Coca-Cola by citing the inclusion of lime in the former, there is no basis in this being the truth. In fact, based on David Embury's 1947 recipe, the two drinks were one in the same.

Piña Colada: A Cuban Native

James Bond never ordered one. It is hard to picture Ernest Hemingway setting a frosty one down next to his typewriter. Yet the Piña Colada is the drink of choice for countless cruise ship passengers, sun burnt tourists sporting loud Hawaiian shirts, countless infrequent imbibers, and, in truth, the one of the most broadly influential cocktails ever created. Of course, like many great flavour combinations, before the drink's history began, the Piña Colada has an extensive prehistory.

Literally translated, Piña Colada means "strained pineapple". Minus the coconut, the combination of rum and pineapple dates back centuries. The first record of Europeans encountering a pineapple points to the island of Guadeloupe, November 1493. Sailors on Christopher Columbus' second voyage named the curious fruit "piña" as it resembled a giant pine cone. The native Tainos were already drinking pineapple juice (which they called *yayamaby*) for refreshment and as a digestive aid, especially after consuming meat. Taino women were known to use it as an exfoliant and skin whitener. It was Columbus who brought the first pineapples to Spain. And this exotic fruit enchanted Europe. It was not long before the pineapple became a symbol of wealth and hospitality throughout Europe and the colonies. Ship captains would mark a triumphant return from the tropics by placing a pineapple at their front gate: a gesture adopted from Caribbean tribes. This elegant fruit also became the crowning glory on many upper-class European tables.

Wherever colonial rum and pineapple production took hold, the maceration of the two ingredients soon followed. For example, a traditional digestif in La Reunion, Rhums Arrangés Ananas macerates fresh pineapple, vanilla pods, and cinnamon with white La Reunion rhum.

The same held true for any country that had colonies where rum and pineapple were exported back to the homeland. With Barbados and Jamaica as likely initial sources, Britons went wild for Pineapple Rum.

An advertisement appeared in the 26 March 1783 edition of *London's Morning Herald And Daily Advertiser*. Bridge's on the Strand produced and sold Pineapple Rum for 16 shillings per gallon that was "so much approved for its flavour". Six years later, the company changed hands and was renamed Glanfield's Vaults. But instead of selling simply Pineapple Rum, the new merchant sold the same product, alleging that it was aged for eleven years.

Historian Samuel Morewood, in 1824, wrote that: "The richness of flavour peculiar to this spirit, which has rendered it famous in almost all part of the world, is supposed to be derived from the raw juice and the fragments of the sugar-cane, which are mashed and fermented with other materials in the tun. The essential oil of the cane is thus imparted to the wash, and carried over in the distillation; for sugar when distilled by itself has no peculiar flavour different from other spirits. Time adds much to the mildness and value of rum, which the planters, it is said, often improve by the addition of pineapple juice."[244]

By this time, Pineapple Rum was also very popular in parts of Europe, where fresh pineapple was far too costly for all but the wealthy. Even author Charles Dickens, in 1838, made mention of a hot version: "Mr. Stiggins was easily prevailed on to take another glass of the hot pineapple rum and water, and a second, and a third, and then to refresh himself with a slight supper previous to beginning again."[245]

The recipe was simple as given, in 1819, to housewives to make ample stock for their homes. "An excellent flavour may be given to it by putting into the cask some pineapple rinds. The longer rum is kept, the more valuable it becomes. If your rum wants a head, whisk some clarified honey with a little of the liquor, and pour the whole into the cask. Three pounds of honey is sufficient for sixty gallons."[246]

Piña con Ron is a familiar dessert in Spanish homes. Sticks of peeled pineapple are sautéed until golden in a little oil. Removed from the heat, rum is poured over, which deglazes the pan and creates a rich sauce. But the same phrase also refers to a popular beverage. Jugo de Piña con Ron or simply Piña con Ron [pineapple juice with rum] is the perfect afternoon cooler. The same drink goes by other names. It was called Piña Fria or Piña Fria Colada, by the early 1800s,

244 S. Morewood, *An Essay On The Inventions And Customs Of Both Ancients And Moderns In The Use Of Inebriating Liquors* (1st edn, Longman, Hurst, Rees, Orme, Brown, and Green 1824) 164-165

245 Charles Dickens and Hablot Knight Browne, *The Posthumous Papers Of The Pickwick Club* (1st edn, Chapman & Hall 1907) 353-354

246 E. Hammond, *Modern Domestic Cookery, And Useful Receipt Book, Sixth Edition Improved* (1st edn, Dean & Munday 1835) 192

especially after Cuban officials commissioned importation ice from Spain and then from New England throw Frederic Tudor.

Once ice manufacturing equipment was developed and adopted on the island during the mid-1800s, ice cold pineapple juice with or without rum could be found from Santiago de Cuba in the east to Havana in the west.

When tourism exploded after the 1898 Spanish-American War, flocks of visitors joined the Caribbean planters and foreign businessmen in sipping frosty glasses of Piña con Ron. American newspapers spread the word about this tropical treat.

However, the American publication, *Travel* magazine, added a new twist when it mentioned another refreshment named Piña Colada: "At the end of almost every bar is a heap of ripe pineapples and green coconuts. An excellent drink is made by mixing the milk of the latter with a little gin and a tanal, a cake of sugar foam. But best of all is a piña colada, the juice of a perfectly ripe pineapple—a delicious drink in itself—rapidly shaken up with ice, sugar, lime and Bacardí rum in delicate proportions. What could be more luscious, more mellow and more fragrant?"[247]

There seemed to be some confusion during American Prohibition about the Piña Colada. Was it a non-alcoholic beverage— Piña Fria Colada—whose name was shortened to Piña Colada, simply because most Americans didn't understand Latin American Spanish? Or was it a mixed alcoholic drink as Irving Brown described?

The appeal for pineapple in the United States was due largely in part to Jim Dole, who in 1901, founded the Hawaiian Pineapple Company, which strove to put the fruit in every American grocery store.

---

247   I Brown, 'Cuba's Vivacious Metropolis' [1922] *Travel*

So the Piña Colada or any pineapple drink was of interest to anyone in mainland America who had experienced the tropical fruit.

Some American journalists offered a temperate view of Cuba's delightful pineapple beverages. For example, author Harry La Tourette Foster, in his 1928 travelogue *The Caribbean Cruise*, wrote that: "For the tea-totaler, there are plenty of non-alcoholic drinks obtainable in most places. In Havana, for instance, a favourite iced drink is jugo de piña or piña colada..."[248]

A *Hartford Courant* reporter similarly stressed the Piña Colada's "non-alcoholic" nature: "Down in Havana, Cuba, there is a soft drink that is very caressing to the esophagus, known in Spanish as either *piña fria colada* or *piña fria sin colada*, which might be copied in the United States where soft drinks are now legion."[249] The reporter then devoted four paragraphs explaining how to order Piña Fria, Piña Colada, and Piña sin Colada from a Cuban café "bartender".

But it does leave one to wonder if this was just politically-correct editing. One *National Geographic Magazine* article mentioned the Piña Colada as non-alcoholic in one paragraph and later alludes to its potentially alcoholic nature: "For the thirsty there is the 'pineapple refreshment,' made of freshly crushed pineapple, sugar, and water. Some order it colada, which means strained; others like food and drink together, and order it sin colar (without straining), with the pieces of crushed pineapple in the glass, a real treat. ... In the evening the cafés are busy places. Many of them, continental style, spread out over the sidewalk. There the people sit, sip their drinks, smoke talk, and watch the passers-by with thorough enjoyment. One practically never sees an intoxicated Cuban, despite the fact that they drink much wine and beer. ...The poor people are the

---

248 H.L.T. Foster, The Caribbean Cruise (1st edn, Dodd, Mead & Company 1928) 27

249 The Hartford Courant, 'Traveler Ecstatic Over Cuban Drink' (1922)

most patient and law-abiding I have ever know. I have sat at a side-walk café table, surrounded by well-dressed, well-fed people, sipping a piña colada...and listening to an orchestra of flashing-eyed beauties play and sing their native music with its strange, yearning rhythm."[250]

Since it first opened in 1817 as La Piña de Plata [The Silver Pineapple], Bar La Florida's drink speciality was pineapple juice. Success continued even after its changed its name, in 1867, to La Florida. That tradition continued, in 1898, when Don Narciso Sala Parera took ownership, and again, in 1918, when Constante Ribalaigua Vert succeeded him. In fact, the blend of rum and pineapple appeared more than once on its menu:

FUEGO LIQUIDO
1 ounce pineapple juice
Juice of ½ lemon
1 ½ ounce Carta Oro Bacardi.
Shake with cracked ice.
Fill glass with Hatuey beer and garnish with pineapple and lemon ring.[251]

HAVANA BEACH (SPECIAL)
½ pineapple juice
½ Bacardi
1 teaspoonful sugar Cracked ice.
Shake well and strain into cocktail glass.[252]

---

250   E.C. Canova, 'Cuba—The Isle Of Romance' [1933] *National Geographic*

251   Bar La Florida (1st edn, Bar La Florida 1936) 32

252   Bar La Florida 38

Another drink, the Havana Special, appeared on drinks menus that was of Cuban origins that replaced the grenadine found in Fred Kaufman's Mary Pickford with maraschino liqueur, which was a signature ingredient in Constante Ribalaigua Vert's drinks repertoire.

HAVANA SPECIAL

1 ½ oz pineapple juice
1 ½ oz Havana Club Rum
1 tsp maraschino
cracked ice
Shake well and strain into
a cocktail glass. Garnish with
a slice of pineapple.

It's difficult to say that one thing has anything to do with the other, but it is interesting to note that when this drink appeared in bars, hordes of tourists arrived from New York to take the boats in Key West, Florida aboard the train known as the *Havana Special*.[253]

Operated by the Florida East Coast Railway, this train service offered travellers first-class accommodations and radically reduced travel time to cover the 1,596-mile journey from New York's Pennsylvania Station to Havana via Key West, Florida. From there, the rail service's steamships transported passengers in six or seven hours to Havana. Opened in 1912, the 42-hour, all-Pullman-car service included fine dining and a lounge car. Air service provided by Pan-American Airways, beginning in 1929, shaved the total trip to 36 hours.[254] Even though a Labour Day hurricane decimated the Miami-to-Key West segment of the line, in 1935, the *Havana Special* was in operation until 1960.[255]

253   Hector Zumbado, *A Barman's Sixth Sense* (1st edn, Cubaexport 1980).

254   'The Havana Special' (American-Rails.com, 2016) <http://www.american-rails.com/havana-special.html> accessed 2 February 2012.

255   ibid.

Journalist Charles H Baker Jr [*see left*] discovered an interesting twist in the Piña Colada family whilst travelling to San Salvador, in 1934, where he was introduced to Leche Preparada Piña ["Pineapple Milk"].

PINEAPPLE MILK

Pineapple, sun-ripened until good and soft, juice and pulp
1 Vanilla bean, 2 inch long piece; or 1 tsp extract
Good sound liqueur brandy, 1/2 cup or so; or white Bacardi
Milk, 3 cups
Sugar, brown, to taste; white will do
Pineapple is topped, pared and sliced off core. Then either chopped into small piece or crushed in a mortar until almost pulp—saving all the rich juices. Blend everything together, let be for two hours, and serve well chilled and garnished, if in the mood, with incidental slices of orange, pineapple, sprigs of mint, or maraschino cherries. It is a grand how weather potation, and has been known to cause chronic invalids to take up their—and other—beds and walk.[256]

Obviously the palate for pineapple and rum with a creamy balance had certainly taken hold in Central America.

Another new twist on the ubiquitous rum and pineapple beverage was reported, in 1950, to have its provenance in Cuba—the Piña Colada: "Drinks in the West Indies range from Martinique's famous rum punch to Cuba's piña colada (rum, pineapple and coconut

---

256   Charles H. Baker, Jr., *The Gentleman's Companion: Volume II, Being An Exotic Drinking Book Or, Around The Word With Jigger, Beaker And Flask* (1st edn, Derrydale Press 1939). 91

milk)."[257] Where did this correspondent find this drink? The official 1948 *cantineros'* manual contained only a non-alcoholic recipe for chilled and sweetened pineapple juice under the title "Piña Colada".

Far more important than the first collision amongst rum, pineapple, and coconut in a blender is the drink's transition from ignominy to ubiquitous cabaña libation. Who standardised the Piña Colada into the drink that we all know today?

The Piña Colada has been described as sickly sweet, a dessert in a glass, a beginner's drink. But like many other classics, it has stood the test of time because in the right time and place, prepared properly, it can be the perfect drink for that moment. The time and place might be mid-afternoon in a South Beach hotel swimming pool, or on the in the shade of an ocean-side cabana flanked appropriately by coconut palms.

It is generally accepted that this creamy version of the Piña Colada was introduced in San Juan, Puerto Rico, on 15 August 1954, at the Caribe Hilton's Beachcomber Bar [*see right*].[258] The resort was still relatively new. Opened on 9 December 1949, with its prime

---

257   The New York Times, 'At The Bar' (1950) 271

258   Caribe Hilton, 'Caribe Hilton, Birthplace Of The Piña Colada, Celebrates The Cocktail's 50Th Anniversary' (2004). Year confirmed through interviews with former Caribe Hilton staff. This date has been variously reported as 1957 in previous press materials.

beach front location and modern amenities, the hotel drew an affluent, international clientele: John Wayne, Elizabeth Taylor, José Ferrar, Gloria Swanson and a host of others stayed there. Joan Crawford even declared the Caribe Hilton's Piña Colada was "better than slapping Bette Davis in the face."[259]

According to the Caribe Hilton press materials, Ramón "Monchito" Marrero Pérez invented the drink, saying that he spent three months developing a cocktail that captured "the sunny, tropical flavour of Puerto Rico in a glass."[260]

Ricardo Gracia, another Caribe Hilton barman hailing from Barcelona, was quoted in numerous articles as the drink's creator. A member of the hotel's bar staff between 1952 and 1970, Gracia explained that he was making one of his creations as a welcome cocktail for hotel guests.[261]

Gracia's Coco Loco was a rum, coconut cream, and crushed ice concoction that was served in a hulled-out coconut. One day, the pickers who gathered coconuts from the trees around the resort went on strike. The hotel had received a large shipment of pineapples so he hollowed out a few and served his Coco Locos in them. He loved

259   'Birth Of The Piña Colada' (Frommer's, 2005) <http://www.frommers.com/destinations/ sanjuan0323027721.html> accessed 2 February 2005

260   Monchito was also known as "Moncho" by his friends, according to Norman Parkhurst, former manufacturer of Coco López. Jared Brown, Interview with Norman Parkhurst, 'Telephone Interview About The Invention Of Coco Lopez' (2005). "Caribe Hilton 50th Anniversary" promotional card distributed in 2004.

261   Jared Brown, Interview with Ricardo Gracia, 'Telephone Interview About The Piña Colada' (2005)

the pineapple flavour and accentuated it by adding pineapple juice. Then he named the drink for the strained pineapple that he added.[262]

Hector Torres also joined the Caribe Hilton, in 1952, working first as a bar back and then as a bartender. When asked who invented Caribe Hilton Piña Colada, there was no hesitation in his voice, "Monchito!" According to Torres, Gracia was his and Monchito's supervisor. As such, Gracia was undoubtedly present at the drink's birth.[263]

Miguel Marquez, who worked as a waiter, headwaiter and maitre'd at the hotel, also states that Monchito invented the Caribe Hilton Piña Colada. According to him, Torres had already taken Gracia's place as Monchito's supervisor. Marquez also agreed with Torres that most of these early Caribe Hilton Piña Coladas were served in tall glasses, garnished with a pineapple slice. However, he pointed out that some were served inside pineapples or coconuts.[264] Score one point for Gracia.

Torres also remembered the Coco Loco, though he recalled making it with rum, apricot brandy, coconut water, and a little Coco López. According to him, the mixture was vigorously shaken and strained into a coconut.[265]

A plaque at the entry of the Barrachina Restaurant in Old San Juan proclaims that in 1963 Ramón Portas Mingot invented the Piña Colada. Legend has it that Mingot was too shy to approach a beautiful customer, so he created a special cocktail for her based on

---

262 Jared Brown, Interview with Ricardo Gracia, 'Telephone Interview About The Piña Colada' (2005)

263 Jared Brown, Interview with Hector Ramón Torres, 'Telephone Interview About The Piña Colada' (2005)

264 Jared Brown, Interview with Miguel Marquez, 'Telephone Interview About The Piña Colada' (2005).

265 Jared Brown, Interview with Hector Ramón Torres, 'Telephone Interview About The Piña Colada' (2005)

improving a pineapple, coconut, and rum that farmers and fishermen had enjoyed for some time. She became his wife and true to all legends they lived happily ever after.

But eyewitness accounts from Torres and Marquez date the Piña Colada's birth and naming in 1954, nine years before Mingot mixed his love potion at Barrachina.

When asked during a phone interview who invented the Piña Colada, Gracia replied chivalrously, "We did. Monchito, me, Hector Torres, Carlos, Roger Lopéz, Enrique. We did. The Caribe Hilton crew was like a family. You want to know who invented the Piña Colada? Just remember one name: The XXXXX"[266] As for the Barrachina's claim, Gracia said, "The bartender there worked for me at the Caribe Hilton before he worked at Barrachina."[267]

One claim frequently ignored by most cocktail authorities is that Coco López catapulted the Caribe Hilton Piña Colada out of obscurity. This appears to be true. Certainly, the Puerto Rican Piña Colada would not exist, much less become widely adopted, if not for commercially prepared cream of coconut.

A common cooking ingredient throughout the tropics, but very labour intensive to prepare, cream of coconut was automated and packaged as Coco López, in 1954, by Ramón López Irizarry, an agricultural professor from the University of Puerto Rico. Irizarry personally approached bartenders and chefs around San Juan, encouraging them to experiment with his new creation.

The Coco López company then continued to spotlight the Piña Colada in its promotional literature for over thirty years, spreading the

---

266   Jared Brown, Interview with Ricardo Gracia, 'Telephone Interview About The Piña Colada' (2005)

267   ibid.

drink around the world. It finally found its way into the *Mr. Boston Deluxe Official Bartenders' Guide* sometime between 1970 and 1972.

The Caribe Hilton Piña Coladas were not all made in an electric blender. During the mid-1950s, the Caribe Hilton employed 49 bar employees and three or four electric blenders, according to Hector Torres.[268]

He related the following as the original recipe and method of preparation if a blender was not available:

CARIBE HILTON PIÑA COLADA (TORRES VERSION)

A cup of shaved ice
4 ounces pineapple juice
1 ½ ounces white rum
2 ounces coconut cream
Combine all ingredients in a shaker. Shake well. Strain the mixture into a frozen 14-ounce Collins glass. Then add the shaved ice directly from the shaker. Garnish with a chunk of fresh pineapple.

According to Gracia, here's the original recipe:

CARIBE HILTON PIÑA COLADA (GRACIA VERSION)

One fresh pineapple
One green coconut
White Rum One cup
Crushed ice
Pour the juice of the coconut into blender. Add a scoop of the coconut's jelly. Chop off the top of the pineapple and set aside. Hollow out the pineapple using a pineapple

268   Jared Brown, Interview with Hector Ramón Torres, 'Telephone Interview About The Piña Colada' (2005)

cutter and place contents in a blender. Mix pineapple and coconut well. Add the rum. Add crushed ice and blend five minutes until creamy.
Pour Piña Colada into the hollowed out pineapple. Make a hole in the top of the pineapple for a straw,close and serve.[269]

In Gracia's words: "It's very important that it's creamy. Some bartenders add too much ice and it becomes a sorbet. It's not a frozen drink. If it's frozen, it's nothing. Creamy, creamy!"[270]

The hotel did not immediately add more electric blenders when Caribe Hilton Piña Colada was invented. As Torres explained, "It wasn't a popular drink when it was first introduced. No one had heard of it. Monchito would make up batches and pour them into three-ounce glasses. Then he would give these away to customers. When they finished, they would usually order a Piña Colada. He worked hard to introduce people to Piña Coladas. We all did."[271]

Miguel Marquez said that Monchito and other staff members would encourage departing customers to remember to order Piña Coladas whenever they returned to Puerto Rico.[272]

Today, the Piña Colada is still the Caribe Hilton's most popular cocktail. And there are definitely enough blenders to handle the demand. The recipe has now been standardised as follows:

269   Jared Brown, Interview with Hector Ramón Torres, 'Telephone Interview About The Piña Colada' (2005)

270   Jared Brown, Interview with Ricardo Gracia, 'Telephone Interview About The Piña Colada' (2005)

271   Jared Brown, Interview with Hector Ramón Torres, 'Telephone Interview About The Piña Colada' (2005)

272   Jared Brown, Interview with Miguel Marquez, 'Telephone Interview About The Piña Colada' (2005)

CARIBE HILTON PIÑA COLADA (2004 VERSION)

In a blender,combine:
2 ounces white rum
1 ounce coconut cream
1 ounce heavy cream
6 ounces fresh pineapple juice
1 half cup crushed ice
Blend until smooth,about 15 seconds.
Garnish with pineapple wedge and maraschino cherry.

Nearly all Caribe Hilton-style Piña Coladas are now made in electric blenders. Though the blender was invented before Caribe Hilton Piña Colada, its rise in popularity, like that of Coco López, runs roughly parallel to this particular version of the Piña Colada.

The brightest musical spotlight that ever fell on a mixed drink was Rupert Holmes' infectious love song "Escape (The Piña Colada Song)" from his *Partners in Crime* album that hit number one on the US music charts in December 1979 and January 1980. This tune cemented the Piña Colada's position in the minds of a generation of young Americans as the ultimate casual, decadent, romantic indulgence. (As the lyrics say, "if you're not into health food.") Those twenty- to forty-somethings, interestingly, are now the forty- to sixty-somethings, who make up the bulk of the cruise ship business.

Holmes admitted that he had never tried a Piña Colada before he wrote and recorded the song. In fact, his original lyric had been "If you like Humphrey Bogart", not "If you like Piña Coladas". He felt that he'd used movie references in enough songs, so he considered using a drink instead. Holmes recalled his moment of inspiration, "When you go on vacation to the islands, when you sit on the beach and someone asks you if you'd like a drink, you never order a Budweiser, you don't have a beer. You're on vacation, you want a drink in a hollowed out pineapple with the flags of all nations and a long

straw. I thought, 'Let's see, there's Daiquiri, Mai Tai, Piña Colada—I wonder what a Piña Colada tastes like I've never had one.'"[273]

This was the last song recorded for the album. Holmes wrote the
lyrics the night before the recording session. He sang the song beginning to end in the morning when he arrived at the recording stu-
dio. This recording was to be a "scratch track" for the lead guitarist's
work. In subsequent recordings Holmes could not match the spon-
taneity and energy of that recording, so the final vocals on the album
were recorded in the first take, the first he ever sang the song.[274]

The composition started with the working title "People Need Other People" and was originally released on the Infinity/MCA record
label as "Escape." The record company added the parenthetical
subtitle later because people were calling radio stations requesting
"the Piña Colada song". MCA was losing record sales because of
the confusion.[275]

If Holmes had never tried a Piña Colada, how did it come to mind?
One possible source is Warren Zevon's May 1978 hit "Werewolves
of London", which included the line: "I saw a werewolf drinking a
Piña Colada at Trader Vic's / His hair was perfect."[276]

The year 1978 was a landmark for the Piña Colada outside the music
studios, too. On 17 July 1978, Governor Rafael Hernandez Colon of
Puerto Rico issued a public proclamation, making the Piña Colada

---

273   'Escape (The Piña Colada Song) By Rupert Holmes Songfacts' (Songfacts.com,
2005) <http://www.songfacts.com/detail.php?id=2896> accessed 2 March 2005.

274   ibid.

275   ibid.

276   R Webb, 'Story Of The Song: Werewolves Of London, Warren Zevon (1978)' Independent (2008)

the national drink of Puerto Rico. Monchito attended the ceremony, as did representatives of Coco López, including Norman Parkhurst, who presented the bartender with a colour television set as a token of the company's gratitude.

There may never be a precise answer as to who invented the Caribe Hilton Piña Colada. Was it Monchito? Gracia? Monchito and Gracia?

From Pineapple Rum to the Caribe Hilton Piña Colada, it is obvious that the blend of pineapple, rum, and eventually coconut evolved many times over the centuries.

It is possible that Cuban version was created by a lesser-known, unpublished Cuban cantinero and became popular with American journalists who encountered it.

As with many other cocktails such as the "75", the Aviation, and the Blackthorn, the Piña Colada has a name that was applied to more than one drink by more than one bartender.

But its Cuban provenance as a cocktail is undisputed.

El Presidente: Dedicated to the One in Office

General Mario García Menocal y Deop [*see left, below*] had been Cuba's president since his election in 20 May 1913. He was still in office when the hotel began to welcome dignitaries, celebrities, and masters of industry who visited this isle of tropical hospitality. Is it possible that Eddie Woelke put this drink on the menu to honour a visit from El Presidente?

According to some sources, the drink was first created at the Bar Vista Alegre on Calle Belascoaín, which was built sometime after 1909 when the Malécon's construction reached that area. It is possible that word of the drink found its way into Woelke's ear. He, in turn, finessed it and popularised amongst his elite clientele.

And local lore has frequently noted that this was the politician's favourite recipe before 1921, when he was voted out of office.

When the Sevilla-Biltmore's ten-storey tower wing and grand ballroom were added, in 1924, Eddie left the renovations behind and moved on to the Casino Nacional. (Some people say he also did a stint at the Havana American Jockey Club).

Once again, who knows if he was responsible? But when President Gerardo Machado [*see left*] was voted into office the following year, El Presidente was slightly modified and renamed Presidente Machado.

A slim volume titled *El Arte de Hacer un Cocktail y Algo Mas* was published in Havana, in 1927, by the Compañia Cervecera International SA. There we find Eddie's Presidente as well as a Presidente Machado! What's the difference? Dashes of both grenadine and curaçao are used to enhance the marriage of white rum and dry vermouth in the Machado.[277]

PRESIDENTE (1927 VERSION)

½ rum
½ French vermouth
dashes of grenadine
Stir over ice and strain into a cocktail glass. Garnish with an orange peel.[278]

PRESIDENTE MACHADO (1927 VERSION)

½ rum
½ French vermouth
dashes of grenadine
dashes of curaçao
Stir over ice and strain into a cocktail glass. Garnish with an orange peel.[279]

Basil Woon gave Woelke's El Presidente the highest praise back in 1928, noting that: "It is the aristocrat of cocktails and is the one preferred by the better class of Cuban."[280]

---

277 El Arte De Hacer Un Cocktail Y Algo Mas (1st edn, Compañia Cervecera International SA 1927) 59

278 ibid.

279 ibid.

280 Woon

We know that Machado himself was proud enough of his version to present it to another dignitary: Calvin Coolidge, who was US President during the height of Prohibition. The press was at the scene: "...although the state dinner given by President Machado of Cuba at the presidential palace last night in honor of President Coolidge was exceedingly wet, starting with a fiery 'presidente cocktail' and ending with fine old 1811 brandy, guests at the dinner insisted that President Coolidge did not drink any of the wines or liquors."[281]

American newspapermen at the scene tried to pry more details from guests and officials. But none were forthcoming. So they declared in their columns—without witnessing the dinner—that Coolidge had scrupulously abstained.

El Presidente's and Presidente Machado's popularity continued in Havana's bars even after, in August 1933, Gerardo Machado was exiled to the Bahamas: the aftermath of a bloodless coup that ended with his forced resignation from office.

Constantino Ribalaigua Vert preferred to have his staff garnish La Florida's version of El Presidente with a cocktail cherry:

EL PRESIDENTE (LA FLORIDA VERSION)
½ Chambery Vermouth.
½ Bacardi.
½ Teaspoonful of Curaçao.
Crushed ice.
Cool well and strain. Serve with cherries and a peel of orange.[282]

---

281   The Independent, Evening Edition, 'President Leaves Cuba For Florida' (1928)

282   Bar La Florida 57

Charles H Baker Jr discovered the drink at Bar La Florida later in that decade:

HABANA PRESIDENTE
1 pony each of Bacardi Gold Seal,
and dry French vermouth, into a bar
glass with cracked ice. Donate
1 tsp grenadine and the same of curaçao.
Stir and serve in a Manhattan glass
with a scarlet cherry for garnish. Finally
twist a curl of yellow orange peel over
the top so that the oil strikes the
surface of the drink, then drop the
peel in...[283]

The Cuban bartenders' association took a slight step back to Woelke's recipe and a baby step forward when they standardised recipe in their 1948 edition of *El Arte del Cantinero*:

PRESIDENTE
(1948 VERSION)
½ vermouth Chambery
½ rum
spoonful of grenadine
Stir over ice and strain into
a cocktail glass. Garnish with
a cherry and an orange twist.[284]

After Prohibition was repealed in 1933, Eddie returned to New York where he presided at the Hotel Weylin Bar, bringing with him his talent for working with Cuban rum, which is documented in his 1936 book *The Barman's Mentor*.

283 Baker 99

284 *El Arte del Cantinero* 393

Granted, this history lesson on Cuban cocktails only demonstrates a tiny tip of an immense iceberg that may have begun at the turn of the twentieth century, consisting of hundreds upon hundreds of original recipes. But the story does not end with this history drifting away on the ocean. In fact, the body of work known as Cuban cocktails has grown deeper and extended across Seven Seas with the turn of the twenty-first century.

The Legacy and Future of Cuban Cocktails

Any and every culture is best defined by its living traditions, those beliefs and practices that are passed down from one generation to the next. And in Cuba, the art of the *cantineros* is its heart. That heart is founded on adopting, assimilating, and embracing each new influence and making it wholly Cuban. The passion and beauty that is expressed from weaving so many threads into this cultural fabric excites each and very visitor. In turn, no one walks away from Cuba without becoming an ambassador, spreading the island's cultural assets around the globe.

The body of the *cantineros'* art is deeper than the sea. And although we only discussed in some detail the most famous drinks from this living tradition, there are hundreds more to be discovered, revisited, and revamped from Cuba's Golden Age of Cocktail.

A new golden age of Cuban cocktails has dawned that stands on the shoulders of the drinks giants who came before them and inspire them to weave together threads of individual style and cultural elements from their homelands with the already multi-faceted fabric of the Cuban drink repertoire. With a young, vibrant generation of entrepreneurial Cubans giving rise to paladars and new bars, a new age of inspiration and invention has emerged on the island. Names such as La Guarida, Sia Kara, O'Reilly 304, El Cocinero, Madrigal, El del Frente, and Versus 1900 are surely soon to become the classic establishments of the future, joining hearts, minds, pride, and passions with their famed predecessors.

Joining this community of Cuban drinks craftspeople are talents from the around the world. Some have competed in the prestigious Havana Club Cocktail Grand Prix and represent the broad influence that Cuban rum and the cantinero ethos still have on contemporary drinks menus from as far as Australia and Asia to Europe and the Americas. These new drinks may echo classic concepts. But the final executions are fresh interpretations designed to appeal to modern palates hailing from a broad spectrum of cultural preferences.

CUNYAYA
BY AMAURY CEPEDA ÁLVAREZ, CUBA, 2016 WINNER
60ml sugar cane juice
45ml Havana 7 Años
7.5ml bitter orange juice
5ml honey
5 drops of Bitter Truth Island Fruit
3-4 pieces of ice
Place ingredients in the mixing glass,
stir hard for 6 seconds; double strain into a ceramic
crock filled with ice. Garnish with tobacco leaves, a
sugar cane stirrer, and pair with a lit Cuban cigar.

TRES MEDIOS
BY POVILAS VEILANDAS, LITHUANIA,
2016 SECOND PLACE
50 ml Selección de Maestros
30 ml homemade bay leaf and allspice syrup
25 ml pineapple juice
20 ml lime juice
2 dashes Angostura bitters
Shake ingredients over ice and fine strain into an Old
Fashioned glass. Garnish with 3-5 bay leaves.

CUBAN CYCLE
BY MARIAN KRAUSE, GERMANY, 2016 THIRD PLACE
50 ml Havana Club 7 Años
15 ml vino seco
15 ml fresh lime juice
20 ml homemade coffee-flavoured honey
3 celery leaves
Shake ingredients over ice and strain into a coupette.
Garnish with lime, citrus leaves, and a flower.

ROSA BLANCA
BY ANDREW LOUDON, UK, 2014 WINNER
40 ml Havana Club 3-Year
15 ml fino sherry
2 ml Ricard
4 cloves
20 ml fresh lime juice
20 ml sugar syrup (1:1 sugar/water)
Shake. Strain.

MOMENTO COCKTAIL
BY BENJAMIN FIERCE, AUSTRALIA, 2014 FINALIST
60 ml Havana Club 3-Year
30 ml fresh pineapple juice
20 ml vanilla syrup (home made)
20 ml fresh lime juice
3 dashes Angostura Bitters
Shake. Strain. Garnish with a Cuban frangipani flower.

MANOS ORGULLOSAS
BY KATSUYA TAKANO, JAPAN, 2014 FINALIST
45 ml Havana Club 7-Year
10 crème de cacao
10 ml dry sherry
1 barspoon sugar
1 barspoon coffee beans
Infuse rum with coffee beans for a short time in a mixing
glass. Stir over ice with other ingredients.

Strain into rocks glass. Cover the cocktail and infuse
with the smoke of a cigar for aroma.

THE CARIBBEAN JULEP
BY JULIAN ESCOT, FRANCE, 2012 WINNER
80 ml Havana Club 7-Year
Fresh mint
20 ml homemade Velvet Falernum
5 ml Pimento Dram
Build in a julep cup and garnish with
a mint sprig, crystallised fruit, and spices

The fine art of throwing a drink which Basil Woon so eloquently
described back in the 1920s has been rediscovered and reintroduced
into the international bartending repertoire in the past decade. Just
as Constante amazed patrons at Floridita with his skill at throwing a
drink in a high arc from one container to another. Today's bartenders are applying the same skill to not only blend ingredients with
perfect dilution but to add a touch of showmanship to delight an
appreciative and international audience.

There are other living traditions that are associated with Cuban rum
and its consumption that have nothing to do with cocktails or mixed
drinks and their execution.

Traditions That Never Die

F amily, friends, food, and *sobremesa* [over the table] are the ingredients for a perfect gathering. It is the perfect excuse to
spend time together, to create lasting bonds. This tradition has tak-
en on elements that are uniquely Cuban after it was introduced from
Spanish ancestors. The scene is played out at home, in restaurants or
cafés, at weddings and other family gatherings.

After everyone has feasted on grilled prawns marinated in mojo, roast pork, grilled plantains, avocado salad, and rice cooked with black beans, out come the cigars, cafecitos, and glasses of rum.

While the non-Latino world races from a hastily consumed lunch or dinner to the next appointment or activity, Cubans prefer to sit back, digest, relax, and chat. The pure pleasure of selecting the right cigar to suit the moment, selecting the right aged rum to complement the experience are only the overture to the meditative act that follows: sip a bit of rum, take a puff of cigar smoke, allow the aromas and flavours to combine. Reflect as you converse with others at the table. Repeat until warmth, depth, and lasting memories are felt in your soul as well as in the hearts and minds of those with whom you have shared the experience. No. This is not a waste of time. This is an enhancement of life at its most visceral level.

Another ritual takes place each and every day throughout Cuba. Whether it is at home, in a bar, a restaurant, on a boat, or on the beach, when a fresh bottle of rum is opened the first splash of rum is allowed to fall to the ground whilst uttering the words *"para los santos"* ["for the Saints"]. A native Cuban will perform this humble act anywhere in the world: the place makes no difference. And Cubans are always ready to introduce this ritual of libation to all who visit the island.

"This is our passport", said Trinidad architect Macholo with a humorous note. "We get a lot of applications for naturalisation. When my friends spend a few days at the house, whether they're French, Italians, or Spaniards, they also sanctify the floor with a drop of rum and then another because it's their last day in Trinidad."

Rough statistics say that 310 litres of rum are annually offered to the saints at El Floridita, whilst the cantineros go through 50 to 70 litres of rum per day, making Daiquirís, Mulatas, Presidentes, and other drinks.

This rum libation stems from a santería ritual performed by its believers who revere the Yoruban deity Changó, the Sky Father, the god of drums, thunder, and lightning; a master dancer, drummer, and patron of music. Changó embodies passion, virility, and power. "Without rum I cannot worship Changó, you see. And if I don't honour my saint at least once a month I will be damned. I need Changó just as much as I need the rising sun each day," Havana resident Angelito confesses. He spills a few drops to sanctify the ground before a small altar to the deity that rests in a corner of his room. Then he takes a sip from the bottle, to additionally "give rum to the saint."

Some people say it is because all Cuban men are sons of Changó—the god who loves all women. It is because of this that they know a thousand ways to tell a woman she is beautiful. Not surprisingly Changó's Catholic counterpart is Saint Barbara, a patron who guards against lightning and protects those who work with explosives. One story narrates that Changó had to dress as a woman to flee from an enemy who intended to kill him. Maybe that is why Changó is frequently invoked and revered because communion with this deity helps an individual overcome powerful enemies.

Cut to another scene.

Angelito is at the apartment of a *santeró* [priest] dressed in blue and gold robes. More than a dozen white-clad worshippers are gathered. Those who are asking for Changó's protection wear necklaces of alternating red and white beads. On an altar, there is a *batea*, a shallow wooden bowl with a lid in which Changó resides. Offerings of plantains, okra and cornmeal porridge, palm oil, and bitter kola are placed there for him to eat. The aromas of Jericho rose, cedar wood and sarsaparilla waft from a metal bowl.

Once Changó has consumed his meal, the revelry begins. Drums play in the background, played by white-clad musicians, while the congregation sway to the mesmerising rhythm. If they are fortunate, one of the assembled with receive Changó's spirit. He will speak to some of them. He will bless them with a *toque de santos* [saints' touch]—a touch to the forehead. He will take a sip of rum and spray it on their feet, protecting them from harm and filling them with passionate love.

As you can now well imagine, there are only a scant few spirits that engender such fervour and reverence as Cuban rum, amongst Cubans themselves and amongst rum lovers around the world.

A NEW CUBAN DAWN

Epilogue

Cuba is an entity unto itself. Yes, it shares the cross-cultural core that is found in larger nations such as the United States, Canada, Australia, and Great Britain. But unlike these major powers, this island nation has gone beyond welcoming the numerous cultures that have landed on its shores. Cuba finds the essence of a migrant soul, embraces its uniqueness, and intricately synthesizes its finest facets into the true Cuban soul.

The media loves to emphasise Cuba's past and the living vestiges that can be seen everywhere: the vintage cars rumbling down the streets; the World Heritage sites such as Habana Vieja, Trinidad, Cienfuegos, Viñales, Santiago de Cuba, and Camagüey; plus living traditions such as hand-rolling cigars and spilling the first drops of a freshly opened bottle of rum "para los santos". But what it does not celebrate with the same enthusiasm is Cuba's inherent talent to learn from its past whilst it carefully plans its future, and the understated vibrancy of the culture today.

Look at how Cuban rum was born. In an attempt to capitalise on extracting value from the waste of sugar production as well as identify a cheap domestic alternative to importing expensive Spanish brandy, Cuban rum had its beginnings. Not willing to settle with an unmarketable product, Cuban planters looked elsewhere for inspiration: from British and French colonies who had already established profitable rum markets; from French filtration and distillation inventions that were both labour-saving and product-enhancing.

Determined to establish a sustainable market even during wars and economic crises, Cuban planters expanded their interests beyond sugar and rum, creating a massive market for molasses which was sold to the world's largest rum producer—the United States.

Equally determined to supply nations in which there was a huge demand, Cuba supplied rum to France at the height of its two worst disasters—the Oïdium blight and the subsequent phylloxera outbreak—as its café society was exponentially expanding from the elite and bourgeois sorts to the working class who wanted inexpensive but quality spirits.

It also supplied more than a few nations during times of war—times when grain was allocated for the demands for bread. Rum was needed to supply the military with rum rations that were part of standard supply call.

Cuba found an additional use for its spirit base, investing in the development of industrial alcohol for use as a fossil-fuel alternative to lower the carbon footprint and support local enterprise. By the late 1920s, Cuba was 95% free of imported fossil fuels.

The bar owners and bartenders of this island nation strove for improved practice and service standards before barmen from other countries supported the concept that survival of the industry is based on professionalism. Their dedication to this belief inspired a global effort to improve the level of respect and quality of service that is now being echoed today.

The classic drinks that were divined from recipes either introduced from other cultures arriving on the island (eg. Daiquirí, Mojito, El Presidente, and Cuba Libre) or ones that were wholly inspired on the island. These have continued to serve as a base for new creations that are being developed around the world. Just look at the output that comes from close to fifty nations at the biennial Havana Club Cocktail Grand Prix!

Is the past just the past, something that we nostalgically address out of a romantic desire to relive and replicate what has gone before? Or is the past a legitimate stepping stone upon which the present can be tested and analysed for its value in the future? Arts & Crafts movement polymath William Morris put it best when he wrote in his 1893 preface to Robert Steele's's book *Medieval Lore*: "In short, history, the new sense of modern times, the great compensation for the losses of the centuries, is now teaching us worthily, and making us feel that the past is not dead, but is living in us, and will be alive in the future, which we are now helping to make."

Truth is, our job in the present is to study what has happened in the past and to ensure that we rescue it "from the enormous condescension of posterity". We must look at Cuban rum and its drinks as an essential stepping stone to the beverage profession's future..

Bilbiography

Alexander J, 'Islam, Archaeology And Slavery In Africa' (2001) 33 *World Archaeology*

Anistatia Miller and Jared Brown, Interview with Elio Moya, 'Interview With Former President of The Club Del Cantineros De Cuba' (2008)

Bailyn B, *The New England Merchants In The Seventeenth Century* (1st edn, Harvard University Press 1955)

Baker, Jr. C, *The Gentleman's Companion: Volume II, Being An Exotic Drinking Book Or, Around The Word With Jigger, Beaker And Flask* (1st edn, Derrydale Press 1939)

Bar La Florida (1st edn, Bar La Florida 1935)

Bar La Florida (1st edn, Bar La Florida 1936)

Beachey R, *British West Indies Sugar* (1st edn, Blackwell 1957)

Beebe L, *The Stork Club Bar Book* (1st edn, Rinehart & Co 1946)

Benes A, 'Spirit Of The Bat: The Rum Dynasty: Bacardí' [1996] *Cigar Aficionado*

Bitner A, *Scrounging The Islands With The Legendary Don The Beachcomber: Host To Diplomat, Beachcomber, Prince And Pirate* (iUniverse 2007)

Bonera Miranda M, Oro Blanco (Lugus 2000)

'Breves De La Historia' [2010] *El Coctel Azul*,

Brown I, 'Cuba's Vivacious Metropolis' [1922] *Travel*

Cadet de Vaux A, 'Observations Sur Une Matière Sucrée, Suppléant Le Sucre. Procédes À Employer Pour S'en Servir' [1794] *Feuille du Cultivateur*

Cámara M, *Cachaças: Bebendo E Aprendendo* (1st edn, Mauad Editoria Ltde 2006)

Campoamor F, *El Hijo Alegre De La Caña De Azúcar* (1st edn, Editorial Científico-Técnica 1981)

'Canchánchara' (Es.wikipedia.org, 2008) <http://es.wikipedia.org/wiki/Canchanchara> accessed 23 October 2008

Canova E, 'Cuba—The Isle Of Romance' [1933] *National Geographic*

Carbondale Daily Free Press, 'Yank Bartenders Leaving' (1920)

Caribe Hilton, 'Caribe Hilton, Birthplace Of The Piña Colada, Celebrates The Cocktail's 50th Anniversary' (2004)

Casas B, *A Brief Account Of The Destruction Of The Indies Or, A Faithful NARRATIVE OF THE Horrid And Unexampled Massacres, Butcheries, And All Manner Of Cruelties, That Hell And Malice Could Invent, Committed By The Popish Spanish Party On The Inhabitants Of West-India, TOGETHER With The Devastations Of Several Kingdoms In America By Fire And Sword, For The Space Of Forty And*

Two Years, From The Time Of Its First Discovery By Them. (Project Gutenberg 2007)

Charpentier de Cossigny J, *Mémoire Sur La Fabrication Des Eaux-De-Vie De Sucre Et Particulièrement Sur Celle De La Guildive At Du Tafia; Avec Un Appendice Sur Le Vin De Cannes Et Des Observations Sur La Fabrication Du Sucre* (l'Imprimerie Royale 1781)

Chez Checo J, *El Ron En La Historia Dominicana* (Centenario de Brugal 1998)

Cirillo V, *Bullets and Bacilli* (Rutgers University Press 2004)

Crockett A, *The Old Waldorf-Astoria Bar Book* (AS Crockett 1935)

'Daiquiri' (El Floridita, 2008) <http://www.elfloridita.net/pages/Daiquirí.php?language=en> accessed 23 October 2008

'Daiquiri' (Havanaturbahamas, 2008) <http://www.havanaturbahamas.com/drinks.html> accessed 27 October 2008

'Daiquiri No.1 Natural (Difford's 10:3:2 Recipe) Cocktail Recipe' (Diffordsguide.com, 2011) <http://www.diffordsguide.com/site/main/welcome.jsp?cocktailId=611> accessed 3 February 2011

Dalton H, *The History of British Guiana* (Longman, Brown, Green, and Longmans 1855)

Dampier W and Gray A, *A New Voyage Round The World* (James Knapton 1699)

'Decision Of The Commissioner Of Patents: Descriptive Terms' (The Trade-mark Reporter 1935)

Derla K, 'Disease-Carrying Europeans May Have Wiped Out Native Americans' (Tech Times, 2017) <http://www.techtimes.com/articles/146875/20160404/disease-carrying-europeans-may-have-wiped-out-native-americans.htm> accessed 10 April 2016

Derosne C, 'Improvement On Making Sugar' Patent number US000004108 1845

Diario de la Marina, 'Cooperación De La Mujer Cubana A La Revolución' (1959)

Dickens C and Browne H, *The Posthumous Papers Of The Pickwick Club* (1st edn, Chapman & Hall 1907)

'Disease-Carrying Europeans May Have Wiped Out Native Americans' (Tech Times, 2016) <http://www.techtimes.com/articles/146875/20160404/disease-carrying-europeans-may-have-wiped-out-native-americans.htm> accessed 6 November 2016

El Arte De Hacer Un Cocktail Y Algo Mas (1st edn, Compañia Cervecera International SA 1927)

Elgin Echo, 'Saloon Men Go To Cuba: Twelve A Day Sail For Havana, Says United States Internal Revenue Deputy At Chicago' (1920)

Emmer P, *New Societies: The Caribbean In The Long Sixteenth Century* (1st edn, UNESCO Publ [ua] 1999)

'Enrique Bastante, Campeon Del Mundo' [1994] *Revista EPICUR*

Escalante J, *Manuel Del Cantinero* (1st edn, Imprénta Moderna 1915)

'Escape (The Pina Colada Song) By Rupert Holmes Songfacts' (Songfacts.com, 2005) <http://www.songfacts.com/detail.php?id=2896> accessed 2 March 2005

Fabry M, 'The U.S. Trade Embargo On Cuba Just Hit 55 Years' [2015] *Time* <http://time.com/4076438/us-cuba-embargo-1960/> accessed 12 October 2016

Font A, 'From Chicote To The Kalimocho: A Century Of Cocktails' (2009) 3 *Mixologist: The Journal of the European Cocktail*

Foster H, *The Caribbean Cruise* (1st edn, Dodd, Mead & Company 1928)

Fougner G, *Along The Wine Trail: An Anthology Of Wines And Spirits* (The Stratford Company 1935)

'Frommer's' (Frommers.com, 2005) <http://www.frommers.com/destinations/sanjuan0323027721.html> accessed 2 February 2005

Galloway J, *The Sugar Cane Industry: An Historical Geography From Its Origins To 1914* (1st edn, Cambridge University Press 2005)

Gates Jr. H, 'How To End The Slavery Blame-Game' (Nytimes.com, 2010) <http://www.nytimes.com/2010/04/23/opinion/23gates.html?_r=0> accessed 24 February 2016

Gomez A, 'Obama Lifts Restrictions On Cuban Rum, Cigars' *USA Today* (2016)

Gupta R and Demirbas A, *Gasoline, Diesel, And Ethanol Biofuels From Grasses And Plants* (1st edn, Cambridge University Press 2010)

Haine W, *The World Of The Paris Café* (1st edn, The Johns Hopkins University Press 1999)

Hale E, *The Life Of Christopher Columbus From His Own Letters And Journals* (1st edn, University of Virginia Library 1999)

Hammond E, *Modern Domestic Cookery, And Useful Receipt Book, Sixth Edition Improved* (1st edn, Dean & Munday 1835)

Harlow V, *Colonising Expeditions To The West Indies And Guiana, 1623-1667* (1st edn, Printed for the Hakluyt Society 1925)

'HAVANA CLUB' US Patent 1031651, 1976

Healy D, *The United States In Cuba, 1898–1902: Generals, Politicians, And The Search For Policy* (University of Wisconsin Press 1963)

Huetz de Lemps A, *Histoire Du Rhum* (1st edn, Desjonquères 2013)

Jared Brown, Interview with Hector Ramón Torres, 'Telephone Interview About The Piña Colada' (2005)

Jared Brown, Interview with Miguel Marquez, 'Telephone Interview About The Piña Colada' (2005)

Jared Brown, Interview with Norman Parkhurst, 'Telephone Interview About The Invention Of Coco Lopez' (2005)

Jared Brown, Interview with Ricardo Gracia, 'Telephone Interview About The Piña Colada' (2005)

Johnson H, *The Bartenders' Manual, Revised Edition* (1st edn, Harry Johnson 1900)

Junta Central de Planificación, 'Comercio Exterior De Cuba. Exportación' (Junta Central de Planificación 1960)

Kervégant D, *Rhums Et Eaux-De-Vie De Canne* (1st edn, Editions du Golfe 1946)

Kokomo Tribune, 'Bartenders Leaving' (1920)

'La Historia Del Daiquirí: El Ciclón Del Caribe' (2012) <http://www. historiacocina.com/historia/articulos/Daiquirí.htm> accessed 2 February 2012

Lam R, *La Bodeguita Del Medio* (Editorial José Martí 1994)

Lewis W, *The New Dispensatory...Intended As A Correction, And Improvement Of...* (1st edn, J Nourse 1753)

Lux W, 'French Colonization In Cuba, 1791-1809' (1972) 29 *Americas* (Washington, 1944)

'Monumento Nacional' (Engenho dos Erasmos, 2016) <http://www.engenho.prceu.usp.br/monumentonacional/> accessed 6 November 2016

Moreno Fraginals M, Moya Pons F and Engerman S, *Between Slavery And Free Labor:*

The Spanish-Speaking Caribbean In The Nineteenth Century (Johns Hopkins University Press 1985)

Moreno Fraginals M, *The Sugarmill* (1st edn, Monthly Review Press 1976)

Morewood S, *An Essay On The Inventions And Customs Of Both Ancients And Moderns In The Use Of Inebriating Liquors* (1st edn, Longman, Hurst, Rees, Orme, Brown, and Green 1824)

Murray C, 'Havana Described As An Americanized Old World Place; Who Is Donovan?' *Galveston Daily News* (1922)

Noller C, *Textbook Of Organic Chemistry* (1st edn, Saunders 1951)

'Ordinary Official Gazette Of The Republic Of Cuba' (Ministry of Justice 2013)

Ortiz F, *Contrapunteo Cubano Del Tabaco Y El Azucar* (1st edn, J Montero 1940)

Pacult F, *American Still Life: The Jim Beam Story And The Making Of The World's #1 Bourbon* (J Wiley 2011)

Pagliuchi F, 'How A Filibustering Expedition Was Landed' [1898] *Harper's Pictoral History of the War with Spain*

'Patent #: US000004108' (Pdfpiw.uspto.gov) <http://pdfpiw.uspto.gov/.piw?PageNum=0&docid=00004108&IDKey=EE05C7AC22CC%0D%0A&HomeUrl=http%3A%2F%2Fpatft.uspto.gov%2Fnetahtml%2FPTO%2Fpatimg.htm> accessed 16 March 2016

Paul C, *Farrow & Jackson Limited's Recipes Of American And Other Iced Drinks* (Farrow & Jackson 1902)

Paul H, *Science, Vine And Wine In Modern France* (1st edn, Cambridge University Press 2002)

Pendergrast M, *For God, Country, And Coca-Cola* (Scribner's 1993)

Pérez L, *Cuba In The American Imagination* (1st edn, Univ of North Carolina Press 2008)

Pérez L, *On Becoming Cuban* (1st edn, University of North Carolina Press 1999)

Phillips R, *Cuba, Island Of Paradox* (McDowell, Obolensky 1959)

Pinney T, *A History Of Wine In America From The Beginnings To Prohibition* (1st edn, University of California Press 1989)

Polo M, Yule H and Cordier H, *The Travels Of Marco Polo* (1st edn, Dover Publications 1993)

Ponce Lopez E, 'The Beet And Napoleon' (2011) 29 *Idesia*

Portilla J and Ceccarelli M, *History Of Machines For Heritage And Engineering Development* (Springer 2011)

Portuondo M, 'Plantation Factories: Science And Technology In Late-Eighteenth-Century Cuba' (2003) 44 *Technology and Culture*

Pretel D and Fernández de Pinedo N, 'Technology Transfer And Expert Migration In Nineteenth-Century Cuba' (2013) MWP 2013 UI Working Paper

Pujol L and Muñiz O, *Manual Del Cantinero* (1st edn, Guillermo Librero 1924)

'QUIÉNES SOMOS?' (Alimport.com.cu, 2016) <http://www.alimport.com.cu/?page_id=100> accessed 25 October 2016

Randle J, *Issues In The Spanish-Speaking World* (1st edn, Greenwood Press 2003)

Robinson G and others, 'Process To Deprive Treacle Of Its Disagreeable Taste, And To Render It Capable Of Being Employed For Many Purposes, Instead Of Sugar' [1794] *The New annual register, or General repository of history, politics, and literature, for the year 1794*

Rochefort C and Breton R, *Histoire Naturelle Et Morale Des Iles Antilles De L'amerique* (Chez A Leers 1658)

Saalburg L, 'World's Seven Greatest Bars' [1959] *Esquire*

San Antonio Light, 'Another Free Bar In Havana' (1934)

Sanchez H, *El Arte Del Cantinero O Los Vinos Y Los Licores.* (1st edn, P Fernandez y Cia 1948)

Sanchez H, *Memoria: 25 Años De Labor Del Club De Cantineros De La Republica De Cuba* (1st edn, Compañia Editora de Libros y Folletos 1951)

Simons G, Cuba: *From Conquistador To Castro* (1st edn, St Martin's Press 1996)

Sloppy Joe's Cocktail Manual (1st edn, Sloppy Joe's 1936)

'Smartest Summer Drink' [1935] *The New Yorker*

Smith F, *Caribbean Rum* (1st edn, University Press of Florida 2005)

Smith F, 'Volatile Spirits: The Historical Archaeology Of Alcohol And Drinking In The Caribbean' (PhD, University of Florida 2001)

Sobrino F, *Nouveau Dictionnaire De Sobrino, François, Espagnol Et Latin, III* (1st edn, Delamolliere 1791)

'Spain And Portugal' (Railwaywondersoftheworld.com, 2016) <http://www.railwaywondersoftheworld.com/spain-portugal.html> accessed 1 April 2016

'Sublimus Dei' (Papalencyclicals.net, 2016) <http://www.papalencyclicals.net/Paul03/p3subli.htm> accessed 29 December 2015

Tarling W, *Café Royal Cocktail Book* (1st edn, Pall Mall 1937)

The Daily Gleaner, 'The Future Of Kola' (1892)

The Daily Gleaner, 'Jamaica At The Crystal Palace' (1905)

The Hartford Courant, 'Traveler Ecstatic Over Cuban Drink' (1922)

'The Havana Special' (American-Rails.com, 2016) <http://www.american-rails.com/havana-special.html> accessed 2 February 2012

The Independent, Evening Edition, 'President Leaves Cuba For Florida' (1928)

The Miami Herald, 'Origin Is Disclosed Of Daiquiri Cocktail: One Of Group Of American Engineers Named The Drink At Santiago Bar' (1937)

The New York Herald, 'CUBA. Report Of The Herald Commissioner, Mr. AB Henderson' (1872)

The New York Herald, 'INSURGENT CUBA. Herald Special Report From The Seat Of Insurrection' (1872)

The New York Times, 'At The Bar' (1950)

The New York Times, 'LOSES COCKTAIL SUIT: Bacardí Firm Fails To Prove Use Of Its Rum Is Essential' (1936)

The New York Times, 'Obituaries: Jennings S Cox Jr' (1913)

The Penny Cyclopaedia Of The Society For The Diffusion Of Useful Knowledge (Charles Knight, 22, Ludgate Street, and 13, Pall-Mall East 1833)

The Valentine Democrat, 'Cuban War Review. Two Years Of Fighting With Little Result'" (1897)

The Washington Post, 'Wants To Learn Mixology' (1920)

Trader Vic, *Frankly Speaking: Trader Vic's Own Story* (1st edn, Doubleday 1973)

'Transactions Philosophiques De La Société Royale De Londres Pour Le Mois De Février 1743' (1760) 7 *Transactions Philosophiques de la Société Royale de Londres pour le Mois de Février 1743*

Unwin P, *Wine And The Vine* (1st edn, Routledge 1996)

Ure A and Ure A, *Recent Improvements In Arts, Manufactures, And Mines* (1st edn, Longman, Brown, Green, and Longmans 1844)

US Government Printing Office, 'The Statutes At Large Of The United States Of America From March 1897 To March 1899 And Recent Treaties, Conventions, Executive Proclamations, And The Concurrent Resolutions Of The Two Houses Of Congress, Volume XXX' (Library of Congress, Asian Division 1899)

Webb R, 'Story Of The Song: Werewolves Of London, Warren Zevon (1978)' *Independent* (2008)

Woon B, *When It's Cocktail Time In Cuba.* (1st edn, H Liveright 1928)

Wright I, *Further English Voyages To Spanish America, 1583-1594* (1st edn, Printed for the Hakluyt Society 1951)

Zumbado H, *A Barman's Sixth Sense* (1st edn, Cubaexport 1980)

GOVERNMENT PUBLICATIONS

Carioca Rum Company v Coca-Cola Company [1940] Court of Customs and Patent Appeals, Volume 28 (Court of Customs and Patent Appeals)

Heublein v Adams [1904] CCMass, 125 Fed 785 (CCMass)

Fondo Registro De Asociaciones, Leg. 305, No. 54, Exp. 8851

Regulations And Instructions Relating To His Majesty's Service At Sea. (1734)

US Department Passport Application 28483, Passport Application

US Form For Naturalized Citizen, No. 77735 (1917), Naturalization application BIO: Jared Brown & Anistatia Miller

About the Authors

They traced the first use of the word "cocktail" to 1798 on London's Downing Street. They know where the Savoy's Harry Craddock is buried. And to top it off, they know how to distill, ferment, and infuse spirits as well as shake, stir, and throw the drinks made with them. During the course of their 25-year-long collaboration, he inseparable, award-winning, cocktail couple, Jared Brown and Anistatia Miller, have written more than 30 books, including *Shaken Not Stirred®: A Celebration of the Martini, Champagne Cocktails, Cuban Cocktails, The Mixellany Guide to Vermouth & Other Aperitifs*, and *The Deans of Drink*.

Their masterwork, the two-volume *Spirituous Journey: A History of Drink* won Gourmand World Cookbook Awards for Best Drink History in the UK in 2009 and in 2010. Miller and Brown became the first spirits writers to receive, in 2011, the coveted International Wine & Spirits Competition's Communicator of the Year Award. The couple were honoured with the Industry Legends Award at the 2016 IMBIBE Personality of the Year Awards.

These two former bartenders also practice what they preach. Brown is Master Distiller for the multi-award winning Sipsmith Distillery. Miller serves as consultant for The Dark Horse Bar in Bath and the Henrietta Hotel in London.

Miller and Brown were co-founders of the Museum of the American Cocktail with Dale and Jill DeGroff. They were the curators of the restoration of Exposition Universelle des Vins et Spiritueux, a museum of wines and spirits founded in 1958 in southern France.

They live in the Cotswolds with their cat, Kitten.

Lightning Source UK Ltd.
Milton Keynes UK
UKOW07f1538241017
311566UK00002B/2/P